~~HOW DO I GET~~

~~A RECORD DEAL?~~

SIGN YOURSELF!

Benjamin Groff

~~HOW DO I GET A RECORD DEAL?~~ SIGN YOURSELF!

YOUR 2 FREE GIFTS! (AND DISCOUNT COUPON CODES!)

Hello and THANK YOU for grabbing a copy of my book! Before we get started, I have two free gifts for you! This is just to say thanks for being a new reader, especially as this is my first book!

FREE AUDIOBOOK!

First, here's a link to get your FREE "Sign Yourself" audiobook read by myself! Yes, not only can I *write*, but I can read, write *and* speak! I made sure to put my own personal style in the audiobook, along with some additional commentary along the way!

Get the Free Audiobook:
www.benjamingroff.com/audiobook

TEACHABLE DISCOUNT CODES!

(USE COUPON CODE **BOOK20** FOR 20% OFF)

Next, I have a number of digital courses at Teachable, waiting for you to check out. You can find them here:

Teachable Courses
https://benjamingroff.teachable.com/courses

I'm excited to develop these courses and truly hope you might find some life changing value for your music career. As a special gift, you can pick up any of the full length courses for 20% off with this Discount Coupon Code!: **BOOK20**

The course offerings currently include:

Insider Secrets to Hit Songwriting - A culmination of my 25+ years as a music publisher, having signed and worked with over 100+ hit makers. I'll help you unlock the "hit songwriting matrix" so you'll never be able to approach making hits (and listening to them) the same way ever again. The course includes 25 Video modules and 5 hours of content! **www.benjamingroff.com/hit**

The Release Blueprint - You've made your music and are finally ready to self-release, but - now what?! The **Release Blueprint** digital course contains over 70 modules and 10 hours of content, revealing exactly *what* to do *when* with your music release, starting 5-6 weeks out - all the way to release day. This is the exact plan I use for my label at We Are: The Guard. We've had over 100 releases and a couple hundred million streams! Trust me, I've made (and paid for) all the mistakes myself - so you don't have to! In other words - let me give you my actual release plan step by step!! And yes, you *need* a plan. **www.benjamingroff.com/release**

FREE "RELEASE BLUEPRINT" PLAN PDF!

As an additional FREE gift, you can get a preview of the **Release Blueprint** digital course by grabbing the 2 page PDF plan right here:

www.benjamingroff.com/PDF

As mentioned, this is the actual release plan I use for my own label, We Are: The Guard. The plan is a 2 page downloadable PDF taking you through all the steps I recommend in properly setting up your music release.

Again - thank you for being a new reader!
And now... on with the journey!

This book is dedicated to all the hard working, dream seeking, big thinking artists, songwriters and musicians—who have the biggest opportunity ever, right now, in the history of music, to set ablaze their own path and "make it" in the music business (which means—making a living doing what you love).

CONTENTS

PART 1:
FOUNDATIONAL EPIPHANIES AND A MINDSET SHIFT

PART 2:
GET YOUR ASS TO WORK— THE 12-STEP PROGRAM

PART 3: SECRETS IN DOING IT

PART 4: FIN

PART 1

FOUNDATIONAL EPIPHANIES AND A MINDSET SHIFT

INTRODUCTION

Prince just asked me to play ping-pong.

Not kidding. It was 2015, and I was at Paisley Park in Minneapolis, as the third of a three-person team to meet the purple one. Long story short (except for Prince's platform heels), the meeting turned out to be one of the most epic encounters of all time ... for *me.* I'm not sure what Prince thought.

And that's when I figured I might have achieved *some* type of success in the music business, LOL. Fortunately, I was able to have two other meetings with Prince, but no, Prince and I never did play ping-pong—I took the advice of his manager, who just said, "Forget it. He'll destroy you." #BiggestLifeRegretEver. But a big takeaway from that experience was how I saw Prince doing things his way. He didn't, as far as I can tell, wait around in Minneapolis and hope someone would sign him or shop a record deal. He made a music and cultural commotion, and the labels showed up at his doorstep—even back in 1975.

Prince's music was, and continues to be, historically incredible, vibrant and vital. He had the utmost sonic and visual identity. He wrote amazing and epic songs. And from what I saw from my own personal experience, he didn't just have a passion for music. He had an obsession.

This is going to be you.

Or at the very least, if you really want to make it, this is the mindset and framework you need to be working within. I'm hoping I can help save you hundreds of hours and help dramatically shortcut your process in making it in today's music business. And, *hint,* this isn't going to be what you thought, as far as making it is concerned.

Thus, the first lesson of the book begins.

It's simply time to reprogram.

In today's record business climate, asking the question "How can I get signed?" or "How do I Get a record deal" is simply the wrong question to ask. It's just so circa 1990s, '00s and '10s. Let me bring you into the 2020s, where instead the *statement* should be "Sign Yourself."

Read on, and welcome to my world.

Benjamin Groff

Owner, Brill Building Music Publishing, 1997–current
Owner, We Are: The Guard – Label / Blog / A&R Resource, 2008–current
Executive VP of Creative, Kobalt Music Publishing, 2006–2016
Snr. Creative Director, EMI Music Publishing, 2001–2006
Creative Manager, BMG Music Publishing, 1996–2001
Assistant / Song & Library Manager, Polygram Music Publishing 1994–1996
Assistant / Song & Library Manager, Rondor Music Publishing 1993

1

FLIP THE SCRIPT

It's time to start doing things differently right now.

The record business simply is not living in the '90s, nor the '00s or the '10s anymore. It's changing rapidly. It seems like every three to six months, there's a new way, a new platform, a new strategy to get your music out there and heard.

Don't worry though. If getting a record deal is one of your key agendas, I *will* tell you how to get a record deal, but first you have to start with the right question: "How do I 'make it'?" And isn't *that* the multi-million-dollar question! Or is it? Perhaps it's the $50,000-a-year question.

But here's the thing: Getting a record deal in today's world is frequently being shown to not even be necessary. Perhaps making $50,000 a year and doing music full time is, in fact, truly making it in today's music business. Is making it being able to quit your Starbucks barista job or the nine-to-five soul-sucking office gig to do music full time? Following your passion—isn't that making it? Of course, making a million bucks and having Top 10 hits would no doubt be incredible; however, being able to do music full time is certainly what I would call success.

In fact, getting a record deal at an early stage of your career, when you have no real deal and negotiating leverage, might actually be one of the worst moves to make! I know too many artists who got discovered, took that early record deal, and got caught up in the mishmash of A&R (artist and repertoire) with flaky executives; and/or nine to twelve months later their A&R person got fired or took another job. It's so sad, but many of those artists just got left behind, dropped, or even worse—that spectacular album the artist put his or her entire life effort into was just left on the shelf without an internal executive champion. It's major record label purgatory.

There are a shocking number of artists' projects sitting in the vaults that will never see the light of day. But I digress. Let's cheer up. There's a much better way to do all of this. "How do I get a record deal?" is still the question I hear the most, yet today it's 100 percent, in my opinion, the wrong question to ask. As I said, we need to reprogram and readjust our question to the following:

> "How do I make the right music that causes a reaction, builds a true fan base, garners real online metrics, creates the fire, and sets in motion a literal *panic* with the major labels trying to sign me?"

Yes, I'm talking about *flipping* the script.

Repeat after me!

> I am *not* going to ask the labels to sign me.
>
> I *am* going to create the buzz myself to where the labels come banging on my door.

Yes and yes! That's how to do it! But it's also a ton more work and takes maybe many years of dedication on your side. And you have to be ridiculously great. But that's okay, because you're in this to win this, right?

And the following is super, super important:

Today, labels are not taking risks. Period.

History Is Not Repeating

Throughout most of the twentieth century, record labels *would* invest in artists and develop them. It was a huge investment, and artists needed labels because only labels had the bucks to advance artists the money for a proper recording studio, video(s), promotions, tour support, etc. They literally needed *at least* $100,000+ to make and market a quality, viable product. And there was no YouTube, Spotify, or Instagram back then, let alone MySpace or Friendster. It took *at least* another $100K just to manufacture, promote, and market an album, let alone create a fan base.

Today, record labels *just are not risking capital/money*. And they certainly are not developing artists, in my opinion. Overall, the labels have decided that because new artists don't need expensive recording or video budgets anymore, the labels can just sit back and see which artists rise to the surface before they quickly move in, pounce, sign them, and throw some proverbial gasoline on the fire of what's already working. Look at it from their perspective. *Why* should they take a risk and do all the work when they can let someone else, aka you, spend the initial investment and work through trial and error, research and development?

Your strategy needs to piggyback on the mindset of the A&R executives. And what is that mindset exactly? Well, if you haven't guessed it already—strap yourself in. Today—signings are rarely inked just on the premise of an executive's "gut" creative feeling. Nope. Today, artists are signed on (sometimes regardless of talent) the "right" data showing up i.e. proof of your music project not just showing signs of life but exploding. It's kind of sad—but true.

However, make no doubt, you can absolutely, 100% use this to *your* advantage. Assuming you're already making great music, this book will show you how to create the metrics the labels are looking for. If you do this correctly—trust me, your inbox will be *overwhelmed* with record label, music publishing and management offers, all in a *panic* to sign you.

The New Mantra

Record labels are no longer signing artists. Record labels are signing existing *business plans.*

Sure, the labels are signing great artists who make great music, but these days it's a requirement for the early work to already be done (and done by you). This book is going to show you how exactly to do that. So let's focus on:

a) making the best music that
b) creates the right buzz and consequently
c) turns into a great business plan and profits that

d) shows up as the right metrics that
e) makes the majors want to sign you!

If you're really in it to win it, you can likely achieve everything and more discussed here. Use the methods in this book to get there. Ideally, if things are working for you, you might at some point even wonder if you need a record label. Well, unless you're looking for your songs to be taken to commercial radio, that answer might be *maybe not.*

Sorry, folks, I don't make the rules, but the sooner you switch your mentality to a DIY (do-it-yourself) approach and get a buzz happening, the sooner the record labels will be knocking on your door. *And that's exactly what you want!* You want to flip the script and have *them* chasing *you* instead of the other way around.

AWESOME!

Hopefully I've hammered that into your new psyche and approach to the music business.

You're now automatically ahead of almost every new artist, so congratulate yourself. I'm serious! You just avoided spending two to three years of your life chasing record labels, during which you would likely be told (if you were even lucky to get a meeting): "Yeah, this is really good. Let's stay in touch to see how things go." Real life translation: I'll call you when I see and hear your project is already happening and taking off.

As you can guess for yourself, this is going to take a lot of hard work, but don't worry. I'm going to show you step by step how to do things. I'll lead you to the proverbial water and introduce you to the online tools and resources that can help. I want you to focus your talents on making and recording and performing music, and also on aligning yourself with new music business partners that can handle a lot of these DIY elements.

Again, please keep in mind that becoming successful today means

- more work,
- more initial investment, and
- more of a commitment from you than ever before.

The huge upside is that you have *complete creative control* over everything! (Prince would be proud.) No one tampers with your artistic direction, your release schedule, etc. You don't have to ask permission for anything, and at the end of the day, you call all the shots.

This is 100 percent different than being signed to a major record label that owns you, owns your masters, usually tells you what type of record to make, decides *when* your album comes out, or *if your album will* ever *come out!* (This is shocking, but it happens—a lot.)

So have you switched to your new mindset? Great!

Summary

Your new mantra and crux of this entire book: Record labels are not signing artists. Record labels are signing working business plans, which exist because of the great music you're going to make, your early hard work, and the buzz you've created.

You're going to make it happen for *your*self.

p.s. Make no doubt, there will be hopefully in your career, a great time to actually consider signing to a record label—either a great independent or a major. I'll tell you under which circumstances you should really consider that, later in the book.

2

THE NEW MODEL OF MAKING IT IN THE MUSIC BUSINESS

Making a living on five million streams per year.

Continuing our fireside chat. Making it in the music business today is not about having a fleet of Ferraris. Nope; today it's about making a living doing music full time, living your dream, *freedom,* and not having to work a crappy coffee barista job that starts at 6:30 a.m. every morning.

You might be thinking, *How the hell do I go about doing that?* First, you're going to be releasing your own music. Assuming you are ready for it, start getting your music up on the streaming and downloading platforms. You don't need a record label anymore because in today's world, *you* are the record label—which is actually the slogan of Kobalt's digital distribution platform AWAL: "I Am My Own Label." You'll never really know if there's love for your music until you put it out to the universe and see what reacts. Yes, in the words of Steve Jobs, real artists ship.[1]

What It Means to Make It

From the '70s to the '00s, the phrase "making it" conjured up images of posh living in Beverly Hills, a small fleet of exotic cars, and living the highlife with caviar and champagne. These days, things have changed quite a bit. Making it is simply about making a living full time doing what you love—making music. If you have accomplished this and can do it year after year, you've won. Sure, we would all love to have that mansion in the hills, but it's also important to have realistic goals with the big dreams.

Your first *realistic* goal to making a living doing music full time is, in my opinion, garnering five million collective streams on Spotify, Apple, Tidal, Amazon and the like per year. Notice I didn't mention Soundcloud, because in my opinion, Soundcloud really doesn't pay out like they should (c'mon Soundcloud). Also, YouTube—you can be doing much better in royalty payments :)

Yes, you *can* do it. Yeah, there might not be a Ferrari in your driveway *yet,* but if you're making a living doing music, that's *amazing!* And you're also building up to bigger and better yearly salaries, and hopefully some good tax liabilities too , LOL. Let's look at the math.

Making a Living on Five Million Streams Per Year

Five million streams, if you own the master recording, is approximately $22,500 in revenue, because one million streams on Spotify earn royalties of around $4,000–$4,500 (check out StreamingRoyaltyCalculator.com for approximate values). Along with those numbers on the streaming side, you might likely also have some synch revenue—which are fees for the use of your songs in film, television, video games, ads, internet, etc.—of about $5,000 minimum, assuming you can get paid both on the master and the publishing.

Sounds good so far. Let's add some live revenue and merchandise into the mix earning about another $2,500—a conservative number. Also, maybe you've put out an exclusive special-edition vinyl piece or have some other miscellaneous revenue coming in. Then there are also ASCAP/BMI, SoundExchange, and publishing royalties adding another $5,000–$10,000 to your yearly salary.

Adding all that together, you might have $40,000 of revenue or more. I know that's not crazy megabucks, and you also have to subtract your *costs* for equipment, attorney fees, marketing costs, other personnel and players fees, mastering, and more, but you're probably able to make your music in your home studio for free. Most importantly, this also means you're not spending draining hours working away at a soul-rushing nine-to-five desk job (or two twenty-five-hour temp jobs, etc).

This means that all your time is devoted to doing music! Priceless. I really do mean that. Forty hours a week (the standard full time job) times fifty weeks per year (assuming you have 2 weeks off for vacation) is two thousand hours a year doing something you *love* instead of something you *hate*. Hmm.

But wait, there's more.

Additionally, you're building a catalog of masters and publishing assets that will pay you back in dividends. That's right—songs you created and released years ago will still be paying out to you in the present day! As a personal example, I recently had a number one hit in Japan that I wrote. I finally got it placed and recorded, but it took *seventeen years* to find the right artist to record and release it. That's probably longer than some of you reading this have been alive. As another example, an artist whose single I released two years ago, and which we were struggling to recoup, only just had his first juicy $30,000 synch come in.

It takes time. It's all about building a robust music catalog. And you can't readily do that when you're putting two thousand hours a year into your lame office job instead of into building your music career.

Supplement Your Income

You might also be able to supplement your income by doing some arranging or production work. Maybe you play in a cover band on the weekends, sell your beats on Splice, busk downtown, or give guitar lessons on the weekend, which at least generates enough to pay the electric bill each month. Or much more—when I went to Berklee College of Music, busking was literally offered as a career choice. There are people who are *amazing* at it and earn a six-figure income tax free (shh, don't tell anyone). It's also how Justin Bieber got started. All in all, you *can* make a living *and* live your dream making music full time. The idea here is you want to be making a living doing what you love—making music. This allows you to focus on your artist or multiple artist projects.

Let me give you an example.

I work with an amazing artist, writer, and producer, Mac Montgomery. Mac's the guy behind two artist projects: DENM and FMLYBND. Each is a different and unique project and thus, Mac has a solid royalty stream, including some great synch revenue, from both projects, as well as touring revenue. Mac also writes and produces for other artists and receives a music publishing advance from myself. He doesn't yet have a Ferrari, and that's not his dream car anyway, but he's making a living in the music business, and the big wins are on the way.

As mention, you can also sell beats, if that's your thing.

> Lil Nas X wrote "Old Town Road" himself using a beat he bought for just $30 on the online platform BeatStars.
>
> BeatStars is a digital marketplace that allows producers to sell their original beats to artists. Producers pay a monthly fee to use BeatStars and get to keep 100% of their sales revenue when artists buy their beats on the platform. The company has paid out over $50 million to producers since 2012, CEO Abe Batshon told CNBC Make It. Batshon said that the music on BeatStars ranges from $20 to $200 for a non-exclusive contract, with increasing prices for more exclusive rights.
>
> A 19-year old from the Netherlands known as YoungKio created the "Old Town Road" beat, incorporating a sample from the song "34 Ghosts IV" by rock legends Nine Inch Nails. Lil Nas X purchased the beat in 2018 for $30, which came with limited distribution rights. After the song exploded in popularity, the pair negotiated a new contract, said Batshon.
>
> Carmin Chappell, "'Old Town Road' is now the longest-running No. 1 song—and the beat Lil Nas X used only cost $30," CNBC's Make It

In truth, there are plenty of totally independent artists and musicians I know earning north of $250,000 a year doing what they love, and in some cases, this yearly income is much more. I always say that artists, songwriters, and Wall Street bankers have one thing in common—they can both make $1 million per hour. Yes, it's the truth! *You* can actually write a career song or smash hit with just *one hour of work*. Some of the biggest songs ever were written that way. So value your time (and I'll tell you how to maximize your time and leverage yourself in later chapters). Or, you can put in those 2,000 hours working at Starbucks. Hmm.

Summary

It is really important that you see that focusing on your music career gives you the space and the opportunity to make your pinnacle works of art. Really, there's no upper limit. By working day and night, year after year, you're creating a catalog of music and songs, and those little babies are out there perpetually working for you.

3

YOUR 1st 1,000 TRUE FANS + OBESSESSION

Distinction—Your first 1,000 TRUE fans are not your first silly 1,000 followers.

If you have one thousand *true* fans, they alone can likely support your career, in my opinion. Finding them will take absolute hard work, perseverance, and brilliance on your part, but keep in mind that these fans will be your viral amplifiers. In other words, these fans will be the ones telling everyone how great you are. I'm not talking *casual* fans here; I'm talking about *true* fans who'll drive five hundred miles or more to see you live. Make no mistake, this is where it starts.

Probably after the *true* thousand-fan mark, you'll start getting some nice traction, evident by your music spreading via your fans' word of mouth. If all goes well, you'll get calls from the record labels, and if you're lucky, music publishers too. And when that time arrives, you can decide if you even need a record label.

It depends on the artist and the music, but you might need ten or twenty thousand followers to find your true diehard thousand fans. From there, a core thousand-person fan base can quickly turn into five, ten, twenty-five, or one hundred thousand and beyond. *These* are the people who will buy *everything* you put out. They'll get every T-shirt, buy every special edition release, and go to every show. They're also, as mentioned before, your amplifiers, and they will shout from the rooftops about your music. These people are the beginning of your army.

Obsession—Your Fans' and Yours

I absolutely look for this quality in any signing I'm considering. And I'll tell you how I came to this realization.

I was watching *Black Swan* starring Natalie Portman. In the movie, Natalie portrays an incredible ballerina who goes to the most unimaginable lengths to make it in her career. She desires to be perfect. Throughout the film, I'm thinking, *Hmm, who is this? Jeez, this reminds me of someone I know. Damn, who is this person?* I couldn't put my finger on it until toward the end.

Of course! This is a caricature, mindset and mold of absolutely every successful artist, writer, producer, and executive I know and work with in the music business.

It's not just good enough to be passionate. In my opinion, to make it to the top of *any* business, you likely need to be *obsessed.* In other words, are you obsessed enough about making your dreams come true, and about your art, to work ten- to fourteen-hour days almost every day for ten to fifteen years? Because it's those Type A people you're competing with.

You might think someone like Taylor Swift has it on easy street, but counter to what you might think, the biggest stars like her put in the longest and hardest hours. Without exception, everyone I work with puts in ten-plus hour days at least six days a week. And really it's usually more than that. So if you want to compete and have your star rise, you need to step into the obsession club. And lucky you, the obsession club is open all hours, day and night.

If you're not obsessed, that's *totally* fine; however, it's important and crucial to realize exactly who you are and manage your expectations accordingly. If you're not obsessed, you can *totally* do music and have success along the way, but it might mean you don't have the star-studded career you're imagining. And hey—you might get lucky. But in my experience, you can't expect anyone to be obsessed about your music and your career, if you are not.

How do you know you're obsessed? Well, if making music is the *first thing* on your mind when you wake up and the *last thing* when you go to sleep, and all other hours in between, then I think you have your answer.

Summary

It all starts somewhere, and that somewhere, as far as making a living pursuing music full time, is (in my opinion) generating about five million streams per year and/or finding your first true thousand fans to support you. You need to focus on creating that foundation first.

The rest follows.

4

THE NECESSITY OF HATERS

If no one is hating on you, you're doing it wrong.

You need these foundational epiphanies and mindset shifts before you really get into the nitty gritty of doing the work to get your music ripping up the playlists, hopefully the charts and racking up those 100 million streams+. You might be surprised that all this foundational mindset stuff, in my opinion, is more than 50 percent of the battle to get there.

One More Foundational Mindset

If you *only* have people generally liking what you're doing, and no one's leaving any derogatory "you-suck" type of comments online, you're probably doing it wrong.

Ummm. What?

I learned this little concept from a music analyst—the most powerful music blogger and overall music and cultural commentator on the planet, Bob Lefsetz.[2] *Huh? I thought the goal is for everyone to* love *me.* Wrong! If everyone simply, generally, casually likes you and thinks you're pretty good, it could actually be the worst thing for your career. In my opinion, you want to avoid being just good at all costs. Even being *very* good can place you at the end of the day in the unremarkable category.

Because with fifty thousand-plus releases *per day,* no one really cares about your new, very good artist project that doesn't provoke any emotion or reaction. Random likes mean you haven't made a strong enough *statement.*

You need diehard fans, people who *love* your music. When you have *that* strong of a message in music, you'll find that for every ten people who *love* your music, you're going to have at least one out of ten who hate or strongly dislike what you do. And just like Tony the Tiger once said (another reference probably over your head, but hey, I try)—more haters? That's *greatttttttt!* If you indeed receive some snarky or even harsh comments online, *rejoice in that,* because it means you may actually be doing something right! Of course, you don't want to have the flip side of this, e.g., two or three positive comments for every ten negative ones.

When it comes to haters, they'll have no problem finding you and expressing their discontent in the comments section on YouTube, Twitter, and Instagram. So if you do get some negative comments on your YouTube video, or a bad write-up in a review, between all the good ones, you should actually feel solid or at worst neutral about it. It means you're doing something right—you're creating a real statement and you're receiving a reaction.

A lot of these trolls are just angry, discontent individuals who think their opinions matter, so whatever, bro. The best and biggest artists have *always* had this going for them, like Lady Gaga, Barry Manilow, NWA, Howard Stern, Madonna, Nine Inch Nails, XXXTenacion, Yanni, Nickelback, Taylor Swift, Bob Lefsetz, Justin Bieber, Marilyn Manson ... all people who have created a fan base of diehard fans.

Equally, there are also groups of diehard haters who can't stand any of the aforementioned artists. That's a good thing! It means that these artists have a sonic and artistic identity; they are beacons of originality and different from everyone else.

The secret here is so counterintuitive. The wrong approach is to create music with the intention of just fitting in and hoping that no one goes about hating on your music. Don't play it safe! You *have to* take risks to stand out in the crowd.

On that note, one of the worst things I often see artists and writers doing is analyzing the charts to see what's working so they can copy that certain style or trend. How inauthentic is that? Where's the thumbs-down button for that artistic expression? You *can't* make music that everybody is going to like, so make music for *you*—music that you innately *feel* and that your niche, hardcore fanbase is going to be *crazy* for.

The great thing about the state of music and the internet today is that there's a niche and tribe and corner of the internet for everyone. If you resonate the *true reflection* of your art, your new fans out there will find you. Fitting in and conforming and being just pretty good in today's new music business is a disastrous fail. To be successful you *must* stand out *and* you *must* be willing to accept that people are not going to like what you do. As Bob Lefsetz said, if there's no one that strongly dislikes what you do, you're just not doing it right!

So yes, you *need* haters, believe it or not. To have haters is actually a good sign, assuming that you have a disproportionate number of lovers. In fact, when it comes to negative comments, you can flip the script for yourself. You might actually *want* to feel disappointed if you don't find someone giving you a thumbs down. Consequently, if someone rips you apart with a comment on YouTube, maybe there's some truth in there to look at, but you're doing something right. You've created a reaction strong enough that it moved someone to say something in the comments section. In essence, you've fulfilled your job as an artist by evoking an emotion. *Bravo to you!*

Haters Can Help Spread The Word

Back in Howard Stern's radio days, his biggest haters and complainers to the FCC were also some of his most frequent listeners. Go figure. These people were also, in a way, his biggest fans as far as the amount of time they spent listening to his show, and consequently the associated radio ads which funded Howard's show.

Comments

I know way too many artists who see a few comments on their latest upload to YouTube, perhaps even loosely saying the same thing, and those two or three comments unjustly set some wheels in motion too where an artist decides to change the entire style or the song or video. Or worse, they get a few bad comments and they take the video and song down.

Look at it this way. One user comment on your YouTube video like "Nice song but wow, that bass is so loud" or "Meh, don't like this new direction—not as good as the last song!" or whatever can get into your head, making you think the thousand people who have read it think the same thing. Don't let it! I have one artist I work with who might receive one negative comment about a mix note or something small, and on that *one comment,* that artist will be determined to get a whole new mix and master. Not needed. Try to not be super reactive to comments. Now if you get a bunch of the *same* comments, then hey, maybe there's something there, but it's *very* unlikely if it's only two or three.

No doubt, comments are helpful and are often vital in helping with pure objectivity. As an example, how many friends are going to tell you your breath smells to your face? Only your very best friends. And that's also what's so amazing about the cold, brutal heart of the internet and also analytical data on any of your songs or videos. You'll very quickly find out if you've got something or not, while your mommy is still saying you're a genius every time you make a song.

In other words, use negative comments as a barometer. There might be some truth in them. On the other hand, don't go obsessing about your comments. They're good to read for a general compass, but at the end of the day, to each his own.

If you like what I'm saying here, and the proverbial lightbulbs are popping off above your head, the best book on the subject is Seth Godin's book *Purple Cow*. Reading this book was a total life changer and epiphany for me. Just trust me—read it, and your perspective on making and marketing music will never be the same.

I promise.

Summary

Haters. They *will* find you. You *will* get negative comments. Look forward to them, and know that your music is evoking an emotion and reaction that can help grow your reach.

5

THE RIGHT MINDSET

Mindset is probably the most cerebral, emotional, and elusive concept of success.

Mindset is something you can't hear or see. Others might see it in you before you even recognize it yourself. The right mindset will take you all the way to the top of the mountain. The wrong mindset will be an evil demon that will derail you every time. Think of Gandalf on that bridge with his magic staff screaming "You shall not pass!" That, my friend, is your subconscious internal programming.

All things being equal between two artists of equal talent, *mindset* is the reason why some artists turn out to be incredibly successful while others just can't seem to crack it, and the latter frequently end up self-sabotaging themselves. You'd be shocked how often this happens. I've even done it to myself.

On that note, the following is a key concept and brilliant quote I picked up from one of my coaches.

"At the end of the day, we get what we think we deserve."

—Ryan Soave

Whoa.

Think about that. Do you *really* think and believe you deserve success? Do you? I mean ... Do. You?

You might be saying, "Hell, of course I deserve that hit record, amazing career, beautiful house, and a butler." But do you really, *really*, really—in your gut and, more importantly, deep in your subconscious internal programming—believe that? Do you *really* have that correct image and value of yourself? Or did your parents, a teacher, or a caregiver tell you growing up that you weren't good enough and would never amount to anything?

Sensitive trigger warning coming: We all have baggage. Period. We all have accumulated programming in our psyche that is either serving us or not. In some cases, we might believe *consciously* that we deserve success. But *subconsciously* we might have an internal voice and self-guiding mechanism that says something completely different.

HEY! WHOA, WHOA, WHOA, WHOA! Were you just thinking about leaving and x-ing out of this chapter? That could be your subconscious mind trying to protect you. Let me pull you back here. Still here? Good.

We all might likely have some level of conflicting internal programming or negative self talk like:

- You're not good enough.
- You don't deserve good things.
- You're a loser.
- That person probably doesn't want to take a meeting or co-write with you.
- People will laugh and hate your next release.

If you told me ten years ago I had some subconscious negative programming that wasn't serving me in my personal life and career, I would have said, "Get the hell out of town, Buck Rogers." But in my own internal personal growth today, I've recognized these things exist big time. Just like a whale that swims through the ocean for decades and unwittingly picks up barnacles, we have to work on ourselves to stay barnacle free as much as we can. We need to try to be conscious of what's no longer serving us and slowing us down and wash it off.

These days I try to work on myself on a daily and long-term basis to make sure I keep my internal programming straight and on track. Trust me, it's hard work. But it's important work, because having conflicting internal programming can result in things like self-sabotage, no confidence, and the inability to break out of your continual orbit of grind.

Escaping the Grind Orbit

Do the words "grind orbit" resonate with you? Yes, that's what I call it. Do you ever feel like you're in this perpetual grind that just repeats and repeats and never ends? This can be compounded if you also have to work a full-time or part-time job while trying to make it as a songwriter and artist. It's a never-ending struggle. What's worse is you may start to make that grind your identity.

I just know too many artists and songwriters who self-sabotage. They finally see things are *starting* to happen. Maybe a new release is on deck and things are about to take off. Here it comes, their success! They're right on the cusp of breaking out of that massive gravitational pull out of grind orbit, and then

BOOM!

Something happens and their booster rockets fail. Believe it or not, they often do it to themselves unwittingly. This self-sabotage is seen in the form of anything like:

- "I don't like this music I spent the last year on anymore. I'm scrapping the album."
- The band breaks up a week before the release.
- They subconsciously mess up a key co-write or relationship or meeting which was going to be their ticket out of the grind orbit.

Or it could be they've made their *identity* of grinding *so strong*, that their ego *must* keep them in that grind loop. Because hey, working your ass off and being a broke musician is both romantic and heroic, right?

Wrong.

It could be even as simple as having an opportunity to introduce yourself to someone who could change your career and your life, yet maybe the negative self talk will raise its voice with thoughts of *They probably don't want to talk to me. They'll think I'm a weirdo.*

You could instead 100 percent flip that negative self talk to *They are so lucky I'm going to introduce myself to them.* And you might be right! *You* might be the one changing *their* career for the better, but instead you denied them that privilege. Think on that for a moment. The same thing goes with releasing new music to your fans. Is some of this starting to make sense? I've seen and been a part of each one of these self-sabotaging examples with artists and writers. And they'll continue to happen.

There's a famous story of a band called the Brian Jonestown Massacre. They were apparently playing at the height of their career at their biggest gig and were about to get a huge record-setting record deal. The *entire* music industry was at this show. All they had to do was play a decent show and the biggest record contract of the year was theirs. And ...

The band imploded and broke up. On. Stage. True story (or so I've been told and rumor has it).

Self-sabotaging can also show up in smaller actions. For example, artists won't reach out to the important person who could change their life because they don't believe they're good enough. Or they think it wouldn't be cool to ask for help. Or they get into more intense self-sabotaging like substance abuse, or they can't manage their emotional states, leading to other unhealthy outcomes.

Many of the key positive mindsets I've incorporated personally, I received from reading books like Napoleon Hill's *Think and Grow Rich* and Hal Elrod's *Miracle Morning.* It's crucial to believe through and through that you deserve the success you're grinding and swinging for. As Napoleon Hill wrote in 1937,

> BE —> DO —> HAVE.
> First, you have to BE.
> Then you DO.
> Then you HAVE.

Trust me, just reading a book isn't going to make a change overnight. This is a lifelong pursuit. Reading some cool books will help, but often the deep work is really about getting over and destroying your inner demons and crappy programming and rebuilding yourself with positive programming. In many cases, including my own, it may require the help of therapists, coaches, and other ongoing deep-work seminars. One program I highly recommend is Gratitude Training.[3] It's something everyone should do. This program might look pretty corporate, safe, and tame, but it's one of the top three hardest yet most rewarding things I've ever done.

Writing a thousand words on mindset in this book in *no way* does the importance of the subject justice. There are entire careers, eCourses, and books dedicated to the subject.[4] I highly recommend you start working on your mindset right now. Not only will you improve your chances of attaining the most incredible successes, you'll also change your own personal life and relationships for the better and ultimately make the world a better place. Some of us are already on a great path and might just need some course correction to get to our ultimate destination. Others might need a whole new compass and GPS system. And look—songwriters and artists and creative people in general are really complex, and likely a bit messed up too! I know this from being a songwriter myself.

To get in that real slipstream of success, especially long-term success, we all need to get on the same page internally with our mindset; otherwise we'll just be swimming upstream against our own internal programming, which may no longer be servicing us. To have and attract success, you need to believe through and through that you deserve to have it in the first place. Let's break out of the grind orbit together.

Summary

So you read the chapter. Problems solved, right? I wish it was that easy. But it's an exciting road and I commend you on making this journey. Trust me, in my opinion, and from my experience, those I work with who stay on the path diligently through thick and thin and who embrace the right mindset usually get to their destination. See you there.

PART 2

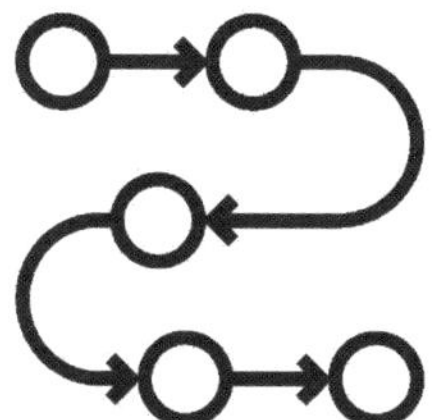

GET YOUR ASS TO WORK—THE 12-STEP PROGRAM

6

THE 12-STEP PROGRAM TO GET THE LABELS IN A PANIC TO SIGN YOU

Time to get to work.

In order of importance, these are the twelve basic steps you need to follow to get your career to the place where the record execs are calling you.

1. Release amazing songs.
2. Clearly define yourself as an artist.
3. Release quality music frequently.
4. Define your social media voice.
5. Create winning videos.
6. Grow your fan base.
7. Get your music on the top DSPs.
8. Develop your marketing plan.
9. Submit your music.
10. Get your music on movies, TV shows, and ads.
11. Develop your unique live show performance style.
12. Grow your team and set up a release day planning template.

And I could add Step 13 here too: rinse and repeat.

QUICK NOTE: This 12-step process, as it relates to massive success, might not work the first time around, and let's be real—it probably won't. Rarely is everyone an overnight success. You have to be prepared to go through all these steps again and again. Bruce Springsteen didn't *really* break out until his third album, and *Born in the USA,* Bruce's biggest commercial album, was his seventh_album! Death Cab for Cutie released six albums until they got to number one on the album chart. Alicia Keys, Lady Gaga, and Katy Perry were all dropped *twice* before they finally got it right. Nearly every artist who had massive "overnight" success usually put in his or her ten years or ten thousand hours to get there.[5]

Keep that in perspective moving forward. This book isn't guaranteeing instant success (nor should it), and you should not expect it after going through this process the first time. It takes hard work, persistence, and dedication to make it. But if you follow the plan outlined in this book a few times over, you'll have, I believe, a fantastic shot at making it happen.

STEP 1

Release Amazing Songs

Please. Don't be average.

I'm always getting asked what I'm looking for or what's going to be the next big thing. The answer for me is *exactly* the same every time. A hit song.

This is the part most people get wrong. They release a safe, normal product with slightly above-average music. Simply put, your music and songs have to be *incredible*, like incredible enough for new fans to sing your praises from the highest rooftops—from their Instagram and other social media accounts.

If you have anything less than amazing music and songs, the techniques outlined in this book will not work simply because being just "very good" isn't worth talking about.

There are about one hundred thousand-plus new releases coming out worldwide every *week*. It used to be seventy thousand releases worldwide *per year,* but now the possibilities of making music cheaply and uploading to the digital service providers are in the hands of everyone; so we need the *wow!* and WTF is this?! and the OMG! level of undeniable music and personal statement from *you.* I call this *fire*-level material.

You need the music to be fantastic so that

a) your new fans will be interested in following you,
b) your new fans will help spread the word to others, and
c) your own music will stand out from the hundred thousand other artists being released that week.

Why "Good Enough" is Actually Terrible

Even artists I work with from time to time recognize flaws in their own songs, production, mixes, etc., but they sometimes default to the phrase "It's good enough." Unfortunately, good enough is going to be your worst enemy. New artists growing their fanbase need to start with *amazing* music and content. In my experience, 99 percent of new artists are just not good enough, nor are the songs well written enough to garner the viral word-of-mouth, "you need to hear this right now" effect. Remember, you're competing with 20,000–30,000 new music releases—per day! You *need* to be remarkable.

To put it in perspective, neither Google, YouTube, nor Facebook, etc. ever had *any* media advertising for themselves in the beginning because these products were *so* extraordinary, they created their own buzz. There was no marketing plan. Their product was so freaking good, the marketing plan was the product itself. You can *and should* do the same!

Make your music and live shows so good, they are worth talking about.

Music Worth Talking About

It doesn't matter if you're Arcade Fire, Kanye West, Britney Spears, or Julio Iglesias; without songs with a capital S, you're just probably going to flounder in the water, or in the case below, sink to the bottom of the ocean/Release Radar playlist of Spotify. Let's hope that's not going to be you.

What exactly does great music come down to? Can great music even be defined? No doubt, you could try to use criteria such as feelings, emotions, or danceability, but at the end of the day, great music starts and ends with songs. Without hit songs you're proverbially dead in the water. I've seen it take about ten-plus years for most hit songwriters to hone a consistent craft. If you aren't a great songwriter, there's no reason why you can't record other writers' material and make it your own. There's nothing wrong with seeking out others who are currently creating the most amazing songs and asking if they have a song you can record. Or, like so many artists who've started their early careers, you can record a cover with a unique, new arrangement. Maybe you're the next Elton John but you need to find your Bernie Taupin lyric-writing partner—that special collaboration that results in the magic. That's 1,000 percent worth pursuing!

The point here is that you need the *best* material. Full stop. And songs are going to be the face of your music. Period.

Perennial Songs

There's no question that songs are *the* vehicles that propel your career and spread your voice through words, melody, and emotion; but you need more than just great songs. You need *hits*, or what I would call perennial songs. As an example, Britney Spears "One More Time" is a hit. And French indie-chill duo Air's song "La Femme D'Argent" is an amazing perennial song. It was never on the charts, but even though it's twenty years old, I still hear it all the time while out and about or used in films/TV shows.

Songwriting

At the end of the day, it's really all about hit songs. One magical song can break open your career, and hopefully you can write more hit songs after that to sustain it. This doesn't happen overnight. You *may* get lucky on your first few attempts, but more likely you'll need to write 100+ songs for a career-making song to effortlessly flow out of you.

If you objectively don't see yourself as a great writer, no problem. Find *experts* at writing songs, writers who live and breathe making great pieces of music, and ask them if you can record their music; or better, co-write with them. John Lennon needed his Paul McCartney and vice versa.

Ideally, if you're an artist, you're writing your own material, but many don't. For example, Frank Sinatra—one of the best singers of all time—demanded only the *best* songs and sought them out. Google "list of songs recorded by Frank Sinatra" and you'll see just how many songwriters he worked with. There was no ego on his part. He just said (spoken in a Frank Sinatra smoothy voice) "Hey,—I need you to be writing dees songzs."

There's no reason why you can't do the same thing, because the right songs are crucial. It's the proverbial jet fuel for your career. So many artists, especially pop artists, had their breakout hits with cover records or songs written by other people. Even Billie Eilish's initial breakout song, "Ocean Eyes," was mostly written by her brother, Finn.

If you are recording a song for the first time and your version will be the first release of the song ever, you *do* need permission from the writers of the song. Make sure to get it, as well as all other important documents and agreements in writing, if needed. Having the right song(s) is the jet fuel to any career. Consequently, it's also when that jet fuel dries up that those superstar airplanes usually fall out of the sky.

I'm sure you can think of more than a handful of artists who just can't get arrested anymore. It's not because they got some wrinkles and a hip replacement. To quote my friend and legendary A&R man John Kalodner, "They just ran out of songs."

Covers

There is an infinite amount of amazing material already released. Why not incorporate that into your song arsenal? You can reinterpret previously released songs and make them your own as a cover. Recording a cover version is not only totally legit, it's totally legal and does not require all-rights-reserved permission from the artist, writer, or music publisher. As an example, Van Halen covered and released singles like "Pretty Woman" and "You Really Got Me." And Patti Smith had a breakthrough rendition of "Because the Night" written by Bruce Springsteen. I repeat, simply releasing your new interpretation of a The Smiths song does not need permission. It's called a compulsory license. You do still need to pay the publisher though.

Trust me, this is not a whole chapter endorsement for cover songs or recording other people's material. I just wanted to put it out there to consider as an option vs. releasing just "pretty good" material. Ideally, you're the one writing the material, so let's assume from here on out that this is the case. Thus, here is the point where the book might end for some people.

I'm. Not. Kidding.

Amazing Songs

If you don't think you have the right, most amazing material yet, there's not much worth in proceeding to the next steps to officially release music, in my opinion. It's more important to spend time and focus on step 1, because only with great material, and great material *only,* will the rest of the steps work. The rest of this book probably won't take you where you need to go. You need the right vessel to carry you, and that right vessel is your *amazing* songs. For sure, you can start building a fan base and garner a little bit of awareness, but having the right music is, I can't say it enough, *vital.*

That being said, keep in mind that if you're not sure about your material or where it stands right now, you can always play in the sandbox of places like Soundcloud or maybe YouTube. You can see what works and what resonates, read the comments, and experiment for free before spending any marketing money. Then, maybe through experimenting and trial and error, when you feel like you have the best material, or maybe a song starts organically taking off on its own on Soundcloud, *then* make that next move and release on Apple, Spotify, etc. You can always keep or delete your tracks on Soundcloud and/or YouTube easily. It's often considered by many artists a safe space to play.

As an example, there's an iconic electronic pop artist I've worked with, who had dozens of earlier tracks up on Soundcloud. When she finally figured out what the "real" first release was going to be, she took everything else on her Soundcloud account down. All those songs and uploads were the bridge to help her figure out what her first *real* official release would be, along with her artist direction. In the meantime, she picked up some early fans along the way. Not a bad plan!

In regards to creating the best material, I've written about perfecting your songs on my songwriting blog, benjamingroff.com/songwriting-tips. The crux of the post is why you need to constantly chip away at your key songs until they are perfect, or as good as they can ever be. It's what I call the "Max Martin Mindset." If you don't know who Max Martin is, he's written all your favorite pop songs. Literally.[6]

Summary

Bottom line: Great songs are the fuel for your career, especially long term. You need the right songs coming from your vessel of *you* in order to broadcast who you are. This will cause your first thousand fans to show up.

STEP 2

Clearly Define Yourself as an Artist

Who is your tribe?

When it comes to finding new fans who are going to love your music, it's totally not what you might think. Or is it? In my opinion, as far as the content you're going to make, it's definitely *not* about going for the juicy, most common denominator and doing what you think everyone's going to like. It's also not about following the trend, and it's *not* about cheesy Instagram likes and tactics. It's also definitely *not* about knocking on record label doors and begging them to sign you. Remember, we're flipping that script to what it's *really* about—making incredible music and remarkable content that's true to you, finding your first true thousand fans, and giving people multiple ways to discover and spread the word about you.

Part of this is embracing what I would call the fringe—that special corner of the internet that's going to embrace and love you for you and you alone. So if darkwave hip-hop goth is your following, perfect. If polka country is your true calling, then that's where you need to head. If you feel like you should have been making music at the height of the '80s on Sunset Strip Blvd., then make *that* music! If your music sounds like nothing else and people can't put you in a box, *that's* incredible. This is another very key part of this book. Don't feel you need to conform, and don't.

Finding Your Tribe

I came to this mini-epiphany about tribes while working with an artist, and though it's not their real name, we'll call them Gothic Toxic. Gothic

Toxic is a dark-goth electronic indie pop project, and if you look them up online, you'll instantly get not just who *they* are but also who their fans would likely be.

While working on their Instagram influencer campaign, the question came up: "Who is their tribe?" I needed to find credible influencers in the tribe and family of Gothic Toxic, if that makes sense. After a good amount of research, I found a company called Upfluence. Upfluence creates software that allows its users to help find like-minded people on Instagram.[7] Essentially, using Upfluence, I was able to mine the data out of Instagram and find Instagram influencers who would most likely support this artist. I did this by searching their posts for hashtags like #goth, #darkindie, etc.; keywords; their number of Instagram followers; their actual engagement; if their profile had an email; etc. Once I had my list, I was able to use Upfluence to manage an email campaign and put the word out on our new singles and give an introduction to the artist. Some of these influencers were happy to just support and spread the word for free. They loved the music. Others wanted a trade, e.g., a post or a story for some swag, and others just wanted a fee.

Early Adopters

But back to my point. I knew musically and *culturally*—key word—who and *what* Gothic Toxic stand for, what they're about both musically and visually. The idea with any artist is to find the early adopters who might be on the same wavelength, and to quote Seth Godin, to find the "sneezers" out there who might be willing to help spread the word. In other words, what "club" or corner of the internet do I need to go to, to find potential new fans.

Here's an analogy. When it came to finding the tribe for Gothic Toxic, it's like as if I was on a crowded city street and a thousand people walked by, I could *very likely* handpick out of that crowd who a new potential fan of theirs might be. It's a lifestyle. It's a look and fashion statement. It's a culture.

On the other hand, take Carly Rae Jepson, who I really like, and her hit "Call Me Maybe." Really, *who* is Carly Rae Jepson? Dunno. What does she stand for? Who is her tribe? I just really don't who she is or what makes her stand out in a crowd. Looking out at a sea of people, I can't really recognize a potential Carly Rae Jepson fan either. Also, what is Carly Rae Jepson's story? I have no idea. I think this is why rappers and hip-hop artists have such a viral and passionate audience—they have created a culture. Or let's look at some other examples. We know what Motley Crue, Post Malone, Notorious B.I.G. (RIP), or Billie Eilish are about. They stand for something. They have a tribe and a true identity.

Visual Identity

For sure, you don't need to look like Lady Gaga or Jon Bon Jovi at the height of his best hair days in 1987, but make no doubt, these people are *stars.* And to that regard, I wouldn't say that Post Malone is a fashion icon ... but wait a minute, I think maybe he is. Certainly, Post Malone is a star in his own right, and there's *no question* he has not just a sonic identity but also a *visual identity*. If I walk by him on the street, I know that's Post Malone. Can the same be said for you?

There is that extra something special about all these people, and their charisma holds that *wow* factor. Mostly, they know exactly who they are and embrace it. Their visual and sonic identity is a direct reflection of that, and when you get yours, magic happens and the universe conspires with you and opens its doors.

Of course, it might be hard for you to objectively quantify if you're a star or not. Maybe you're worried because you weren't born with flawless rock and pop star looks. But looks have *nothing* to do with your charisma. What makes you a potential star is not about the DNA you were given at birth, how high your cheekbones are, or how much you weigh in at. It's about a signature style or look, a signature visual identity for *you.* Think of David Bowie or Elton John's visual statements, or the recent face tattooing craze or even, Bruce Springsteen—with his white T-shirt, blue Levi's jeans, and wood-grained Fender Telecaster—created his own signature visual identity of the Americana working man!

To hopefully *further* prove my point, look at some current stars and icons. Start plugging the names below into Google Search or YouTube. You'll recognize that all the following artists have sonic identity, hits or perennial songs, and a visual identity.

- Run DMC
- Prince
- The Lumineers
- Peaches
- Madonna
- Daft Punk, Deadmau5, Marshmello, Mad Lib, SBTRKT
- U2
- Michael Jackson
- Elvis Presley
- Insane Clown Posse

Here's a challenge. How exactly do you know if *you* have created a visual identity? I look at it this way. It might sound *super* cheesy, but it's 100 percent true. Are you ready? Ask yourself this question: *Can someone dress up like me for Halloween?* Honest to God, it's the question that helps qualify all of this.

I remember signing and working with LMFAO back in the day. Yes, those guys actually roll out of bed that way, it's not just an act. At the height of LMFAO and "Party Rock Anthem," the LMFAO Halloween costume was one of the top-selling costumes that year! You could literally buy a full LMFAO costume package—fully equipped with an afro wig, animal print spandex, and faux diamond-encrusted giant glasses.

Can you dress up like David Bowie or Prince for Halloween? Hell, yes you can. And they are icons. 'Nuff said.

Sonic Identity

You must have a sound and identity that can *only* belong to you.

This means when someone hears your voice or the way you make beats, or your *style* of writing, they know that it can *only* be yours. In other words, you need an identity and a *sound* to your music that no one else has. This is a perfect time for it to all be about *you.*

It's a misconception I see happen all the time. Most people think the road to success is to just follow the crowd and copy what's hot on the charts—a terrible, common rookie mistake. The thinking often is *Oh,* this *song or style is what's happening. I need to be X for people to like me and have success.*

Nah.

You need a sound and identity that's *yours and yours alone.* That's where you create your niche. That's what gets you your first true thousand fans—a number which can turn into ten thousand and then one million; for example: Lil Nas X, ABBA, Michael Jackson, Drake, Joanna Newsom, Metallica, Timbaland, Kenny G, Skrillex, Kanye West, Bee Gees, Miles Davis, Nine Inch Nails...

It doesn't matter what the genre is, they *all* have a sound and style and signature voice that defines *them* and them alone.

Adele at the height of her career was certainly not a Ford Agency model, but Adele's overall vibe, character, personality, voice, and *songs* make her a freakin' superstar! I mean, even beyond the amazing voice and songs, she's someone I would want to hang out with.

Likewise, you need to separate yourself from the crowd and stand for something people can recognize within *three seconds* sonically, visually, and during a live performance. In my opinion, if you don't have this, you might not be able to "pass go."

Finding your sonic identity is also about 100 percent believing and 100 percent recognizing who you *are*, who you're *meant to be,* and what you innately *believe to be true* in yourself. It's likely a sound, a direction, a message, or a style, and it might not even be popular right now. But if you have an idea and a gut feeling of what your identity should be, even if it seems a little crazy, that's what you *should* run to. And the more this sound isn't like anyone else's, the better.

Work on this. Really.

Be Exactly Who You Should Be

As a species, we're really still operating on what I would call Brain Operating System 1.0. Our brain hasn't evolved that much, i.e., we still often have a prehistoric brain mindset. I really believe the new mantra to chant to gain success today is:

"To be safe is to be risky. To be risky and do dangerous work is to be 'safe.'"

—summarizing a Seth Godin presentation[8]

Seth calls our internal resistance to taking risks to having a "lizard brain," because a lizard brain wants you to be safe and fit in. Finding your sonic identity is really about listening to yourself and quieting the lizard brain and the resistance inside you, which keeps speaking up and trying to prevent you from being exactly who you should be. In other words, doing your important work. The lizard brain is also great at coming up with excuses:

- I can't do that. People will think I'm nuts.
- I'll do it after I finish the next semester of school.
- I don't have the right gear yet.
- I'll make that important piece of music once I buy a new computer.
- No one is going to like that idea; it's too left field.

Sound familiar?

Recognize and chase that inner calling rather than accommodating a safer path and what *seems* to be popular right now. It could be that your music and your art will actually change the trend and people will start following your sound. Simply put, when I notice that someone has artistically found the *true* reflection of themselves musically, *that's* when I pay attention, both as a fan and as a publisher/label. Develop and discover who you are as an artist, what you stand for, and then step into it fully. Only then are you likely going to attract a tribe of your similar mindset, your first thousand true fans. Other than your songs, discovering who you are truly as an artist might be the most important step of your entire career.

Speaking to your fringe and making content that appeals to them and yourself is a vital part of the equation. Too many times artists just want to shoot for the juicy center of what's popular now. What they miss out on is the fact that so is everyone else, and guess what? No one really cares about your music that was made for the marketplace, and everyone can spot a fake. Do you want to hang out with that person *trying* to be someone else and resonating nonauthenticity, or would you rather be someone who knows *exactly* who you are and are putting that out to the universe? Give me that absolute original *anytime* over the first.

I could spin so many stories to exemplify this point, but the person who immediately comes to mind is Lady Gaga. It was probably late 2007, and around this time MySpace was the thing. It was also how all us record people were trying to discover new artists, and it was actually pretty great for that. Each artist could have four (if memory serves correctly) songs they could post, and it was an endless rabbit hole of music, for better or worse. The music climate of the time, and the radio plays, was geared toward R&B and urban. That one dance song that would get rotation on KIIS FM in L.A. wasn't played anymore.

There wasn't any Spotify or Apple Play, and maybe barely Pandora, so commercial radio was the shiny ticket (and still is). And while I was on MySpace, I remember seeing a 728 x 90 banner ad for this new artist named Lady Gaga and her euro-pop dance single "Let's Dance." I remember hearing myself thinking *Good luck with that! One hundred percent that's never going to work.* And boy was I wrong. I was framing my opinion based on the environment at the time, which was that radio was not playing any dance/pop, when in fact it was the *perfect timing* for Lady Gaga to arrive on the scene because she was so different!

What would have happened if Lady Gaga had said to herself "Hmm, radio is playing a lot of JLo or Jennifer Lopez or whatever her name is, and if I sing her style of music and add a rapper to all my intros and bridges... I'm gonna chase that sound, cuz that's how I'll be successful." Yeah, I think you know what would have happened. Unfortunately, artists double thinking or doubting their true calling is where the biggest missteps are, and I see people making that mistake all the time. It's a tragedy.

Instead, Lady Gaga was like, if I were to guess, *F*** all that, I know* exactly *who I am, what music I want to make, what I want to stand for, and who my fan base is—however small or fringe they may be at the moment. I'm going to make my music for me and those fans, no matter what.* I think you know the rest. Lady Gaga's music hit the bullseye—not for the mainstream media but for the small sector of people that loved and embraced her. They became true fans. They were brand evangelists and spread the Lady Gaga word with passion.

Today, Lady Gaga has become one of the most important artists in the last ten to fifteen years. On her own, she changed the Top 40 charts in 2008/2009. Suddenly other labels were saying, "Yeah, we need a Lady Gaga too!" Radio was strategizing: "Let's play more pop/dance music. This is working!" Lady Gaga now *is* the mainstream, and she, like Madonna in her prime, now has to continually disrupt herself. Thus, the end of the story and the end of the lesson.

Follow the Positive Thoughts

On that note, I'll give you a hint. That little voice in the back of your head with that very, very special idea, or that glimmer of who you *really* want to be as an artist—*listen to that voice.* There may likely be another, contrary voice inside of you saying "Nah, that's too crazy" or "No one would like that, it's too extreme," or "That's not a music style that's in fashion right now," or "My parents might disown me." Guess what, that artistic direction that feels a little uncomfortable or dangerous—is probably the artist direction you should take. Remember—To be safe is to be risky. To be risky is to be safe.

I guarantee you, with the power of the internet, there *is* a tribe out there for you that will resonate deeply with you, but what you put out there has to be a true reflection of you, who you are, and what you want to say.

STEP 3

Release Music with Frequency, Quantity, and Quality

A constant flow.

So you've got your songs and you've got your identity and who you stand for. Now it's time to think about a release. What should it be? An album? A single? An EP? A 3 pack? Yes, maybe all of the above. This is your show and your plan, but keep in mind the biggest thing—fans want and expect a constant flow of music.

Regular Releases

It's almost like episodic TV. If you've ever watched *Game of Thrones* or *Breaking Bad,* or your favorite episodic TV show, you know that when the show is in season, there's going to be a new episode next week, no matter what. You expect it. We're also conditioned, in a way, to realize that not every show is going to be a home run. Some episodes might be a character-development episode, another might be about plot development. It might not seem like the show is even progressing and then *wham!* You get that home-run episode that knocks it out of the park. And I bet that after that season finale, you might even go back and re-watch some of those previous episodes and enjoy them even more.

It's these home run episodes that usually get all the virality going—people are talking about it, they're coming up with fan theories, their memes are going viral—but it took a bedrock of content for those hits to occur. All those previous episodes laid the foundation and framework for that home run, epic episode to exist.

It's the same with releasing your music. Sure, you want your music to be the best it can be, even if it's a noise art piece, but you need to post a constant flow of music. And you can be sure that Spotify, Apple, and Amazon want to see this too. And if the curators and editorial execs and algorithms at the DSPs (digital service providers) know that you're invested for the long run and that you're frequently releasing quality material, they're more likely to give you a spot on a featured playlist[9], in my opinion.

The Magic Length of Frequency

If you only put out two or three songs per year, *why should* those services help you as much as the artist who's putting out a fresh single(s) every six to eight weeks, which seems to be the magic length of frequency for a lot of the artists I work with. And then maybe when we release the third single in that series, we'll also drop an EP of five or six songs at the same time. Each of those singles will also have a video of some sort.

Don't worry, I'm not talking $10,000 videos here. You can certainly be making amazing, original, "must see" videos on the cheap/mid budget or calling in favors from friends. Feel free to jump ahead to step 5 to learn more about making what I call "winning" videos, as well as some video creation tips and tricks.

Summary

There are no rules on how to release your music; however, please expect your true fans to want frequency and quality. Frequent uploads are an important signal to your fans that you're a viable artist. They can see your latest track was uploaded just last month vs. six months ago. It's also a great idea to stockpile your material and create some goals for the next twelve months of your rollout. Having a written plan on what you're going to do and when can really be crucial when you're trying to hit your targets. I'll get more into that later in the book.

STEP 4

Stay Connected on Social Media—Like Duh?

Plus: Don't make it hard for me to find you. Please keep your shiz updated.

This chapter is super quick and more of an Artist 101 type of lesson, but you'd be surprised how many people get this wrong. It's very, very simple: Please, please have updated social media pages! If you don't have any yet because you still haven't chosen your artist name, read more in chapter 11 about important points to consider before you nail it down.

This book is about how to spark and light the fire for the labels to get in touch with you and beg for *you* to sign to *them,* not the other way around. So make sure you are actually reachable. *Duh!*

Make It Easy to Find You

I know this is obvious, but it'll ensure that when fans, labels, and music supervisors actually discover your music, they'll be able to instantly share it with their friends and also get in touch with you. This isn't just about keeping your social media pages up to date; it also includes having a legitimate email or another way to actually, *gasp,* contact you. You don't want to do all this work and then have a label, or a music supervisor desiring to use your song in a TV show, try to reach out and be unable to contact you. It happens! Also, I would provide a real email address that you check daily versus an internal Facebook, Soundcloud, or Instagram messaging system. Simply put, it's always a bummer for me to find an amazing new artist and I want to start a dialogue, but there's no way to get in touch.

Even if you don't want to put out your real email address, it might be smart to create a manager-type email, even if you don't have a manager. It can help you look more legit. Make it an email that you check every other day. For instance, manager@yourartistname.com.

On that note, there's an interesting and rumored story on Prince that from time to time, he had a management email that he usually responded to, as the actual manager. Who knows if it's true, but I wouldn't doubt it.

Social Media Schedulers

When it comes to social media posting and promoting yourself, yes, it can become a chore. It's sometimes emotionally taxing and time-consuming. Remember when John Mayer canceled his Twitter account because he was spending too much time putting original thoughts and energy into tweeting instead of making great original music?

If you find social media posting is a chore, don't worry. You can always set it and forget it. There are tons of social media schedulers whereby you can upload all your messages, posts, and content for the week in about an hour and it'll automate your posts to all your social media accounts for you. I get more into social media tips in chapter 10.

Is Every Social Media Handle Taken?

This is kind of a joke, but I swear all the best domain names and social media handles—even my own legal name—seem to have been taken, so you might need to get a little creative.

It's great if you can be congruent across all your handles; like, if your artist's name is The Large Coffee, have each handle be @thelargecoffee. Or if that one is taken, then a variation of it works, e.g., @wearelargecoffee.

Which Social Media Platform Is for Me?

All of them! Your true future fans are on every platform. There are people who are more Twitter people and others who are more Instagram or TikTok users. You might certainly find that one platform resonates best for you, but no matter what, make sure your music and your digital voice is everywhere. Reflect *who* you are as an artist within three seconds in everything you post, and have a presence on every social media platform. I've written about your sonic identity and your visual identity. Your digital voice is also an identity.

This is obvious, but it deems stating the obvious. The overall idea is that no matter what, potential fans can discover you on *their* preferred platform, and also *as important*, your new fans can share your music with *their* followers and friends in *their* world. In other words, you may personally not be into, say, TikTok, but it doesn't matter. Your new fans *are,* so help them spread the word on you via their preferred platform. For example, a lot of my artists really *live* on Instagram. That's also where their fans are and that's where they spend 75 percent of their social attention and focus. I have other artists I work with who are all about Twitter, and others who crush it on Facebook. Either and all of those are great! To each her or his own platform.

Keep Checking In

As previously mentioned, it's important to keep *some* type of presence going on all the key platforms, namely, at the time of this writing: Instagram, YouTube, Facebook, Twitter, and maybe TikTok, depending on your potential fanbase. You can always focus on a core platform that you like to use best.

User IDs for New Platforms

Also, don't forget that as new social media platforms arise, you should immediately claim your user ID in case you want to use it in the future. Sure, the "periscopes" of the world might have faded away, but whatever the next Instagram of the day is, you want to make sure you grab your

URL/username early on. I'll talk later in the book about finding a virtual assistant or scheduling apps, as well as setting up your campaigns, uploading your content, and more.

Summary

Believe it or not, if you do things right, people are going to want to get in touch with you, so make it easy. Keep your stuff updated on your socials, and damn, check your email frequently! You never know when all the hard work will pay off and that music supervisor, key manager, or label partner will want to connect to take your career to the next level.

STEP 5

Make Viral "Winning" Videos

And on the cheap!

Creating a viral video is without a doubt the biggest bang for your buck, and the quickest and smartest thing you can do to get instant yet long-term exposure. But first, I should take one step back here. The word "viral video" is, in itself, fairly cringeworthy. And anyone who specifically sets out to make a viral video usually ends up making something seen by only about 1,200 people. So instead of the term "viral video," let's call this the "winning video" chapter. Yes. Winning! Where's Charlie Sheen when you need him?

Make It Fire

Simply put, there are plenty of courageous artists who rolled up their sleeves, put on their "purple cow"[10] thinking caps, went out to make the most undeniably original, inventive, must-share, next-level video, and ended up winning. Conversely, you'd be surprised how many people end up getting this wrong. Their video just fails at jumping off the YouTube screen. Just like most everybody is making "fairly good" music, most everyone is also making just "fairly good" music videos. Bottom line is that nobody cares about their videos or their music.

But what if you were to be brave and do the opposite?

When it comes to making a video, it's just like making music that jumps out of the speakers and into your heart—yours needs to be more original, inventive, smart, and outrageous than 99 percent of other videos out there.

A Million-Dollar Video Idea Does Not Need to Cost a Million Dollars

How about $500? That winning video might only require a $250 camera rental fee and some editing help from your pals. The *idea* here is what's most important. So ask yourself the following: Can that winning, million-dollar idea or concept come from you or someone in your camp—maybe even a fan? Is it an idea you can execute for $250–$1,000? Yes, we're talking about a million-dollar idea that can be made for $1,000 or less.

Yes, it *is* possible. It happens all the time.

Let me restate this. A great, winning video be made for free or for next to nothing, but presented via an amazing idea. When it comes to the right concept, your first twenty ideas and treatments for your video may or may not be good enough. It's important to keep going until you have that "OMG, that would be *incredible*" moment, or maybe even the "OMG, we can't do that, but … hmm, can we?" type of concept. It's *that* one you should jump on—without breaking any laws or doing anything too recklessly dangerous, of course!

What Is a Winning Video?

A winning video is simply a video that makes you want to click that darn Share or Like button, or to grab the URL and email it to everyone in your email address book. A winning video is usually one of the following:

- An OMG storyline or incredibly cool concept
- A highly original, creative idea—OK Go is the master of this, and you can see any of their videos for proof.
- A stunt, or attempting something outrageous, or one that might be in the "can you really do that?" book. Note: I *do not* suggest nor condone nor recommend anything that is illegal or dangerous, but hey, maybe you can hire an insured stuntman?! Or maybe some team already has some crazy, amazing footage they can let you work with … like Spike Jonze, who had this concept on lock in the early stages of his career.[11]

- A one-take video. Many of the best one-take video performances were actually smartly or lightly edited in a few strategic "cut" points. The great thing about the one-take video is that most of the time will be spent in low-cost rehearsal stages like your backyard or basement. Come film day, once this sucker is shot, it's done! There's no editing, just some colorizing and you're ready.
- The bedroom-type performance—often a cover song that conveys the brilliance of a new artist.
- The "WTF am I looking at" video? Enough said.

Examples of Winning Videos, Aka Videos You *Need* to Share

The One-Take Video

OK Go – "Here It Goes Again"[12] – OK Go's famous treadmill viral video. Just. Awesome. Nearly overnight, "everyone" had seen this video. How much did it cost to make? I don't know. $1,000? What did cost a lot is the originality, concept, bravery, and rehearsal time to do something totally brilliant.

What OK Go didn't have to spend in video costs was made up for in sheer originality. Great ideas spread!

OK Go – "This Too Shall Pass"[13] – Ok Go's famous Rube Goldberg Machine viral video. And did you notice the State Farm truck in the beginning shot? Yes, they partnered with State Farm to finance this video.

Spice Girls – "Wannabe"[14] – One of the best music videos and pop songs of all time. While this looks like a one-take video, there are actually a few smart edit points that make the video look entirely seamless. Sure, this one has a much higher production value and costs—having to pay for the location and actors and crew—but at the end of the day, I would guess this entire video was made for $5,000–$10,000, and an iconic, priceless video resulted.

Can you do something similar—all one shot that also resonates with your brand identity and who you are as an artist? That's the other thing with this video—it's also a personality piece. You get the total sense of who these ladies are, their irreverence, and what the Spice Girls brand is about. Girl power!

Matt and Kim – "Let's Go"[15] – Back when I was at Kobalt, I had a lovely opportunity to spend some time with Matt and Kim, who are incredibly great people. At the time, their latest album was coming out, and they had audacious plans to make a video for every song on the album. Today, that might not be so astounding, what with Beyoncé and other artists releasing video albums, but Matt and Kim were one of the first to do that conceptually. I kinda thought, *How the hell are you going to do that? That's like $150,000 of video costs.* Nope.

Words that come to mind regarding this video, and others below, are: Smart. Cool. Original. On brand for Matt and Kim. And no doubt also hella entertaining. How much did this video cost to make? A high-end camera rental and some bucks for the basketball player. No editing. The cost was simply being original and doing something that jumps off the screen.

Matt and Kim have perfected this concept, and many of their videos are original one-take performance pieces.

Matt and Kim – "Hey Now"[16] – Yup, just Matt and Kim dancing. What more do you need, especially with Kim's moves? And okay, not necessarily a one-take video but how much did the video editing and other production values cost on this? Probably close to zero.

Matt and Kim – "It's Alright"[17] – Not necessarily a one-take video, but you get the idea. You don't need $25,000 to make a video that resonates and spreads.

Ibeyi – "River"[18] – At the time of writing this book, the video had almost twenty-three million streams! Not bad for a bathtub video, some water, and a *great* idea. This was a brilliant, artistic piece that was also on brand for Ibeyi, showcasing their artistic style and uniqueness. This video exceptionally captures the "twinness" of them as well.

Keiza – "Hideaway"[19] –_Another amazing one-take video. The major cost on this one is really just having the inventiveness, skill, and time with friends who believe in you to make an amazing one-take video. The video is beautiful captured and professionally shot, so I'm sure there was a cost for the right people and equipment to film, but that's not a bad investment for a video that has 153+ million views. And yes, just like all the other videos previously mentioned, this video absolutely encapsulates everything about Keiza. It 100 percent matches who she is as an artist.

The Stunt Video

Please note, for legal reasons, that I do not endorse or suggest you do anything that is dangerous or law breaking. I'm sure the videos below were captured in safe conditions, barring Matt and Kim being arrested for indecent exposure … and these all have a level of excitement and a *wow* factor that's worth sharing and watching over and over again.

Wax – "California"[20] (directed by Spike Jonze) – Spike Jonze is obviously a genius, and it would serve you well to look at all the videos he's made, especially earlier in his career where budget was likely very tight or nonexistent. But check this video out! Obviously, it's also a one-take video with a stuntman and an epic, ironic ending. In other words, it's not you doing the stunt! The video is a thirty-second, slice-of-life clip of a man, literally on fire, running down an urban street setting. The video is slowed down to 1/4 speed, and as the camera pulls back, we can see all the bystanders going through their mundane lives, completely bored out of their minds. Interesting message, and a winning video for sure.

Matt and Kim – "Lessons Learned"[21] – Yes, Matt and Kim got naked for this one and ran through Times Square in New York City. I'm sure in today's climate they'd get immediately tackled by Homeland Security, but hey, it's a stunt that worked. Oh wait, they were tackled and arrested. Forgot about that.

An OMG Storyline or Incredibly Cool Concept

Dirty Vegas – "Days Gone By"[22] – This is a cheaply made video, but it has a storyline that you *must* watch until the end. Notice that Dirty Vegas, themselves, are in this video—sitting at the picnic table—for only like ten seconds. You don't even have to be the star of your own viral video!

Sick Puppies – "Free Hugs"[23] – This is another extremely inexpensive video, but the important thing is the concept. This is how the popular rock band Sick Puppies got their real first start. At the time of this writing, this video has been viewed over *eighty million times.* Can you make money on those YouTube ads? Yes! I'm sure that Sick Puppies has signed up for YouTube's Content ID advertising network[24] via their YouTube Channel, PeaceOnEarth313.

Young Thug – "Wyclef Jean"[25] – I present you with one of my favorite videos of the last ten years—Young Thug's video for "Wyclef Jean." Apparently Young Thug just never showed up for the video, so the director had to make do with the existing A- and B-roll footage ... minus Young Thug! Then they had to creatively come up with some type of story line. The resulting video is probably ten times better than the original treatment. If I were to guess, I'm sure the original treatment plan was pretty typical and boring. Instead, this video came out as something completely, on its own amazing, worth talking about, great, hilarious, instantly shareable, winning, viral video.

Artists often forget that music videos are essentially miniature films, and films tell a story. Storytelling is humanity's first art form, and as humans, we can't resist a great story.

The Bedroom Performance Video

Lastly, believe it or not, a viral winning video can simply be a stunning rough cut or originally created performance in your own living room, bedroom, or car—performing a cover, or even your own song. Often this is more for pop singers and singer/songwriters, but it works!

Jesse J – "Mamma Knows Best"[26] – This video is from 2009 and showcases the brilliant vocal performance of an early Jesse J. *Wow!* Not only is this an *incredible* vocal performance, but you totally get Jesse's personality. You can't help but love her, especially by the end of the video (watch 'til the very end). The song would later end up on the UK music charts three years after Jesse posted the bedroom video.

Bo Burnham – "I'm Bo Yo"[27] – After millions of spins on YouTube, Bo got a record deal with Comedy Central and his career went off on an upward spiral. This was one of the videos that launched his career. The cost to make this video? Brilliance, originality, and a digital cam. Warning—if you're offended by off-color comedy, do not watch this video!

Pomplamoose – "Single Ladies"[28] – The added benefit of uploading a cover, no doubt, is that when someone YouTubes "Single Ladies," they're usually looking for Beyoncé's version. However, in this case, Pomplamoose's excellent version of "Single Ladies," especially in the earlier days of the song, also comes up high in the search results. To date it's gotten eleven million views. Cost of making this video? Probably just knowing how to use Final Cut Pro[29] and a lot of editing time!

Justin Bieber – "Busking in Ontario, Canada"[30] – I believe this is the video that got every record label, and assumedly also Scooter Braun, his current manager, to track him down and aggressively sign him. And can you blame them? The video appears to have been uploaded in 2007, which would put Justin at just twelve or thirteen years old. The takeaway is that sometimes even an amateurishly captured, grainy video can launch a superstar career.

The "WTF Am I Looking At" Original Video

Simply put, these videos are simply captivating. Sometimes they're art pieces. Sometimes they're uncategorizable. Yet they all fall into a winning category of videos that must be shared.

IamWhoIAm – "15.6.6.9.3.9.14.1.18.21.13.56155"[31] – This track is an example of a highly artistic piece of work that's worth talking about. At the time of release, no one knew who this artist was. There was a high level of mystery within a great concept and a beautiful aesthetic; essentially a piece of video art. The video is overall worth remarking about and thus, the idea spreads. And as a sidenote on the mystery factor—people were trying to guess who the artist was. They were asking if it was Lady Gaga's art project, a new artist entirely, or something else.

TOBACCO – "Human Om"[32] – TOBACCO is an artist I've had the privilege to work with on my publishing roster. I'm sure this video didn't cost a lot; however, it's essentially another great example of a winning video—where originality, weirdness, and a great concept become bigger than any budget you could ever have. You can be sure that this video generated a ton of word-of-mouth advertising by people sharing this weird, amazing video they'd just witnessed.

Bonus: The Winning Video That's Secretly Not Even about Your Music

Huh? But if I make a music video, the video should be about me, *right?* Well, maybe not. Winning videos don't even have to be about you or your band, nor do you need to be in them.

Check out this video created via a completely different industry sector. It's something Ray-Ban put together, and this YouTube video is called "Guy Catches Sunglasses with Face."[33] You would never really know until the end, where the logo "Never Hide" comes up, that this is really a commercial for Ray-Ban sunglasses. I watched this video at least three times and sent it to all my friends, and I bet you might have done just the same.

This video is cool and jaw-dropping, yet totally lo fi. There's no reason why the music behind this video couldn't have been yours. Chances are, you could probably have easily made this video, which has been viewed at least 5.5 million times! You can bet that if there had been a real artist and song behind the video, people would be digging in to find out more and adding it to their playlists and sharing. So take a note from the million-dollar advertising power and minds at Ray-Ban. They made a cheap viral video with a million-dollar idea and an amazing concept. My guess is the only cost was a strong post-visual effects artist.

You can do this as well, the most beautiful part being that your video can spread like absolute wildfire overnight, and it will if it's truly viral. When you have an insanely great idea, the marketing cost to you is nearly zero dollars, because as Seth Godin once said, great ideas spread.

YouTube's Description Field

Before we depart this chapter, I know you know this, but you'd be surprised at how many artists don't utilize the YouTube description field as much as they could. Please use it and leverage yourself. This is the perfect place for your

- Socials
- Links to stream your music
- Website links

- Tour dates
- Bio
- Information about making the video
- The people who helped create the video

Put all that information here.

And don't forget, if you have some new information like new upcoming tour dates or new merch, there's no one stopping you from updating every single video you've ever uploaded at any time with those new links and information. Oh, you're kicking off your summer tour? Put all those tour dates in the YouTube description field. Free advertising. *Kapow!*

Recognize Your Unique Ability and Also Recognize Others'

One last note on making winning videos, and please do take this to heart, as I feel you'll have much better results. Your expertise is in making music, which has taken you years to develop. So why, overnight, would you expect to have similar expertise in shooting, directing, filming, coloring, and overall video post-production methods? Instead, find someone local—someone who's obsessed with making amazing pieces of film. Maybe this is someone at a film college or art school, or maybe it's a friend, or relative who has a strong level of experience with filming. It can also be a trade, i.e., someone you can hire to create a video in exchange for using your music for free in their project. That could really be an ideal trade. Additionally, if you live in a major metropolitan center, there are numerous up-and-coming indie film and indie video directors who are always looking to upgrade their own directing reel. Along with some string pulling and favor asking, often these people can create a $25,000-looking video for $5,000 or less. That's worth exploring as well.

Ultimately, what I'm trying to say is that unless you're out to capture a winning video on your iPhone via your bedroom or backyard, don't expect yourself to instantly be a film or directing expert. Be smart and ask for help.

If you're smart, you'll do this in every aspect of your career when it comes to management, accounting, publishing, and digital marketing. You want people who have been doing this for years and love doing it, and who are experts in the field. Then you can spend more time making great music, which is your expertise.

Summary

So there you have it: six categories of potential starting points for creating your winning video.

1. The one-take video
2. The stunt video
3. The OMG story line or incredibly cool concept
4. The bedroom performance video
5. The "WTF am I looking at" original video
6. The video that's not even about you

Let's get that viral winning video!

STEP 6

Grow Your Fan Base

And do it by providing value.

Part of this journey to finding true fans who help grow your music is making your music *free.* Well, um, your music is already free for the most part, but believe it or not, people still want free downloads and free stuff. If your music is basically free via streaming but you can give something away of higher value, you might as well be getting something for it like an email address.

Let me explain further by first telling you a story. About twenty years ago, I was scouting an artist and went to see her show. I was shocked, because at the end of the performance, she was giving away her CD for free. She'd made with a CD burner and handed it over in exchange for an email address. This was way before giving away your music was at all an accepted practice, much less streaming services being in existence. In fact, it was right about the time that iTunes and downloading MP3s were starting to get in full swing.

Let me try to further frame the scenario for the impact. Giving away your music for free, at that time, was sacrilege; but it turns out this artist was thinking way ahead. Her plan was that for every CD she gave away, she would get in return the email address of a potential new fan. She knew that email address was worth a lot if that person became a true fan—one who might potentially buy everything she released and every piece of merch, and come to every show she played. That's a much higher lifetime value than ten dollars for a CD.

Fast forward to today and music is pretty much free, if you don't mind putting up with some annoying ads. We expect music to be free. Sure, people are still buying CDs and downloads, but if I want to hear Journey's

"Separate Ways" or even one of your songs, I just need to open Spotify, YouTube, or Google Play and click. Obvious.

But let's look at another case study—not just any case study, but a brilliant and successful plan from one of my favorite artists, Trent Reznor of Nine Inch Nails. This is actually an oldie but a goodie. The presentation may be old, but it's fascinating. In this breakthrough model, Trent gave away his *Ghosts I-IV* album, that's four albums, for free! This was before the reign of streaming services, so people were like, "Dude, what the hell are you doing?" The free download included more than thirty-six song downloads of new Nine Inch Nails music.

Trent was able to manage all of his digital assets, create automated links to download the album, build and manage his email database, and also see the geolocation source of the free downloads. He didn't have to set up any servers or know how to program PHP, and he used a service called TopSpin Media[34] to handle it all. The way TopSpin Media works (or worked) is that in exchange for an email, fans received free media: a link to an okay-quality MP3 of the four Nine Inch Nails albums. They also received the option to get different packages or come back later to Trent's website and upgrade to better packages and better MP3 quality. Trent even had a deluxe package of *Ghosts I-IV* limited to 2,500 pieces. These were beautiful deluxe packages with great artwork. They were autographed and numbered, with Blu-ray extras including downloads, two CDs, and more, with each set going for $300.

This deluxe package sold out in two days and grossed Trent $750,000 *instantly.* The *Techdirt* story on this subject is well worth a read.[35] Trent also gave the option to buy the CD, as well as higher digital resolution formats like FLAC and MP3s.

Here's the rub. Later that year, just like a proverbial drug dealer giving away the first taste for free, the number-one digital selling album on Amazon was, you guessed it, NIN's *Ghosts I-IV!* The music was so damn good that people wanted to upgrade from the free, okay-quality MP3s and get much higher quality MP3s or the CD. And by giving away his music for free, not only was Trent able to get new fans hooked, he was also able to get his music in more hands than ever before. The only distribution cost was what he paid TopSpin. The word spread big time. This led to more sold-out shows, more merchandise, and tens of thousands of email addresses. Trent self-released *Ghosts I-IV* in 2008.

And BTW, a recent hit sampled one of those tracks from *Ghosts I-IV*—the longest running number-one single of all time to date—Lil Nas X's "Old Town Road."

I have a question for you. Those emails that Trent collected over a decade ago? How much revenue do you think they have created over a period of ten-plus years from all the NIN releases, tour dates, and merchandise? A whole hell ton of a lot, that's how much. Trent was a genius to dig into this early "free" paradigm. Now Trent can reach those fans on a one-to-one basis whenever. He has countless true fans/qualified buyers who can't wait for his next email, and he can grow his sales numbers without any Facebook or Instagram ad spend. He simply sends an email, it shows up in people's inboxes, and voilà. So yes, given this example, hell yeah: free can be a *huge* business model.

This probably would not have worked if the music was crap and Trent had no sonic identity. Look, he's friggin' Trent Reznor, and he also had a preexisting fan base. But aside from those two things, this is how the new digital music world operates. When you create great artistry and use tools to help your music be discovered and shared, people and fans will come.

There's an amazing and thorough presentation on Trent's exact strategy for *Ghosts I-IV* and his other albums online. Again, this is from 2009, but perhaps "The Michael Masnick Trent Reznor Case Study"[36] will give you an idea for a strategy and thoughts on how you can apply this to your own music. Look it up on YouTube. I'm sure you might get some ideas for your own project, no matter what year it is now.

Building Your Email List

Get your fans' email addresses. I don't care how you do it (ethically) or what strategies you use—but I always (with a sad, heavy heart) do a face palm whenever I meet a new artist that hasn't been building their email list (or SMS phone list!). These are people aka your new fans, who *want* to give you their time and money. And keep in mind, social media services come and go, but direct email has stayed the course. Remember back in the day when you, perhaps (?) built your MySpace followers (that went "poof"), and then—your Facebook audience? Yes, that long-ago fantasy time in Facebook, when you made a post and it reached *all* of your fans and friends. Well, now you have to pay for that privilege to reach everyone via a boosted post. Thanks, Zuck. But—what about email? Love it. Email is amazing because it's a one-to-one relationship. You send the email, it gets in your fans' inboxes, and voilà.

Some people say that Instagram is the new email, but I don't see email going away anytime soon. And there are so many services you can use to manage building your email lists, and consequently, dialogue directly with your first thousand true fans. I'd suggest accelerating your email sign ups by giving away something for free, like a digital download, or maybe by providing something really different, like creating a 15 second personal ditty you can write for them (by using their name) or maybe mail them a personal polaroid, who knows—get creative! You should also have an email collection system interfaced on your website.

As far as services to help manage this, they're always continually changing and evolving, so I'm not going to go into great detail here. A Google search may service you better results at the time of reading this. However, one service that immediately comes to mind is one we personally use for all our label email management at We Are: The Guard: Hive.co. There are also services such as Keap (previously Infusionsoft or "confusionsoft" as we would affectionally call it), Constant Contact, Drip, SendinBlue, and Mail Chimp, just to name a few that you can use.

Please note, though, that not all of these services are created equal. Just getting an email in someone's direct inbox versus a spam folder or a promotions folder in Gmail is a huge challenge. IMHO, Keap has the best industry rate for actually landing an email in someone's inbox, but they're also very pricey. Hive, in our experience has also been really great and has some additional features they've set up with music artists in mind. Let's talk about that and an idea for a strategy.

The Digital Exchange

By using Hive.co (and many other email services) you can easily interface their API with Soundcloud, as an example.

With Soundcloud's Pro account, you can add a button in each Soundcloud song tray next to the Favorite and Share buttons, and you can customize it to say

- WATCH and push people to YouTube, or
- BUY where you can link out to your DSP.

Or (listen up!) you can make this button say Free Download, copying Trent's strategy. When you're linked up with a digital management system and users click that button, they'll be prompted to take an action *before* getting that free piece of content. That action can be just about anything, like a Soundcloud repost or Facebook like. In this case, you can also combine them. Or maybe you just want to collect their email as the action point. Regardless, before they get their free asset, they have to present their email and take one of those actions. Then, and only then, does the download automatically start, or a link is sent to their email address to retrieve the asset. And voila, for a free download, a potential new fan is both following you on Soundcloud (or even Spotify; yeah, that can be an option). *And* you have their email address to alert them to new music, videos, and live shows. Note: Free Downloads—are actually still kind of a thing—depending on who you talk to!

You can do all kinds of things to grow your fan base and start acquiring emails. Contests can definitely be a great idea. For instance, you can run a contest and manage it via your email management system. Once you have the custom-made link for the contest with the details and artwork, you can push this out on your socials. In exchange for an email, offer the chance of prizes like an opportunity to meet you backstage, or an exclusive piece of swag, or a Facetime or Zoom personal concert over the internet, or a chance to ask you questions.

BTW, if you're getting this as an eBook, it's very likely that I used the same strategy: While this book is for sale, I likely gave away a few chapters (or the entire book) for *free* in exchange for your email. You might have then consequently bought the entire book as a physical copy (I hope so!) or maybe a songwriting course because of the freebie. Case in point.

Things can change as the years go by, but I've also used a great service called ClickFunnels.com to manage the electronic delivery for this book. And on very selective occasions, when I have something great to share, I may email you cool stuff from time to time. The idea here is that you're getting emails from me that are not spam. Bottom line—provide value. Always. Especially if you're giving something away for an email.

It also goes without saying, but *you should never ever spam your audience!* You want to send emails that provide value, so much so that your fans *love* getting your emails. If you do this right, your email should be the *first* email they click on that week because you're delivering awesome stuff.

Lastly, we talk about "email" here—but there's a growing trend (and a surprising openness) when it comes to collecting mobile numbers from your new fans. There's also a rise of cool SMS bots and the like to check out. Now, it used to be that cell phone numbers were the *last thing* people wanted to give away. But today—if a fan REALLY wants to connect with you, a cell phone number might actually be something they're quite willing to share—*and* one of the best assets you can acquire in the pursuit of your 1 to 1 fan relationship. There are even artists who will randomly call their fans and say Hi. Now isn't that cool?!

Summary

Bring value! Provide something awesome with your great music for your new fans, and give them a reason to start following you. Leverage your music with some swag or personal experiences in exchange for an email, so you can find and encourage your first true thousand fans.

STEP 7

Get Your Music on the DSPs via Digital Distribution Services

DSPs = Digital Service Providers (Apple, Spotify, Amazon, YouTube, Tidal, Deezer, etc)

Now it's time to finally release your music to the world. Exciting! And perhaps even a little scary. After all, this is the moment you begin getting your music up on Spotify and Apple and all the other 150 streaming and download stores out there. It's probably easier than you think. You'll need to employ the services of a digital distributor like AWAL, Distrokid, or Tunecore; and while it's pretty easy to upload your WAV audio and your high-resolution artwork and set up a release date, there is some additional finesse required to picking the right digital distributor. Depending upon what you're looking for, some are going to be more beneficial than others.

For sake of reference, let's quickly get some definitions out of the way. Digital distribution services are the platforms that help get your music on the digital service providers (DSPs) like Apple Music, Spotify, and Amazon. There's a clear distinction, though, between digital distribution services and digital service providers, and for artists who might be completely new to this process, it's important to make that distinction. As far as the best digital distribution services for *you,* you need to know what you need it to do.

Digital music distribution services will simultaneously submit all your music to all the various streaming platforms, but if you want to get your music playlisted and editorially featured on Spotify, Apple Play, Amazon, etc, you'll need a distribution service that really "gets" you and will make a commitment to "working" your music. Or maybe you're looking for deep data analytics on who exactly is listening to your music and where and how. You see, knowing exactly what you're looking for, as well as the associated costs of each service, will help you hone in on which service will be right for you.

They're All the Same ... to a Degree

All digital distributors, at a basic level, pretty much provide the same core service at the end of the day, which is getting your music on the 150+ streaming services and download stores. They also offer monthly payments of your royalties, as well as some type of information on your data: where your listeners are, what playlists you're on, how people interact with your music, etc. With that in mind, let's take a look at some of the most popular digital distribution services, with thorough reviews for each. Let's start with our favorite and who we currently use for the releases on my label, We Are: The Guard.[37]

AWAL

AWAL[38] doesn't take just anybody, and that's a positive thing. AWAL is unique in that they're a submission-based service. Yes, brand-new and non-established artists are certainly able to apply to AWAL, but look, you've got to be really good; and you'll get bonus points if you have some sort of existing fan base, a social media following, and/or it's clear your overall artist vision is on point. While that may sound daunting, don't let it deter you. Think of it as a vetting process, which means you're guaranteed to be among the most talented artists if you're accepted. Also, AWAL is known for quality, which may help your music get noticed quicker if you have their proverbial seal of approval.

AWAL is also noteworthy in that they don't require any upfront fees; they don't get paid until you do. They take a 15 percent commission, which is incredible compared to the record deals of former years, where you'd be lucky to get 10 to 15 percent of the profit. It's almost like a reversal of fortune in regards to what the artist can receive on a percentage basis in today's age. As a huge plus, if AWAL feel they can significantly move the needle for you, they may serve as your makeshift label, which they do for some of their better-selling artists. They even offer payment advances for top-earning clients, making AWAL somewhere between a digital service provider and a proper record label.

Kobalt Music ultimately bought AWAL, and in my experience as a Kobalt Music employee for ten years, as a hypothetical example, if you're an AWAL client gaining some incredible momentum, let's say as an example:

- consistent thirty to fifty thousand-plus streams a day
- great blog write-ups
- playlisting
- buzz

and you need, say, $10,000 for additional digital marketing, AWAL can see that that's a good bet, and you may likely get your $10,000. That $10,000 advance would mean that someone on the AWAL team believes you can garner the additional 2.5 million streams or so needed for that advance to be repaid. There's often an uplift in AWAL's rates if you take an advance, with fees sometimes going from 15 to 20 percent, but hey, it's likely worth it. Last I checked, you can't walk into Bank of America and ask the teller for an advance against your Apple streams.

Now this brings up a good point. What are your master royalty and label streams actually worth?! To see how much money you can actually make on Spotify or Apple Music, you can use a streaming royalty calculator, such as StreamingRoyaltyCalculator.com.[39] You can choose the streaming service, insert the number of streams you want to calculate, and voilà! For example, if you choose Spotify and put in 2,500,000 streams, and you'd get an approximate value of $10,000. If you do the same and change the service to Apple, you'd get $12,500. That same streaming number with Tidal? $30,000! Things that make you go hmmm (as Aresenio Hall once said. Yet another reference you probably didn't get, but that's okay).[40]

But getting back to AWAL ... AWAL's deep analytics and the AWAL app are *fantastic.* AWAL provides notifications when your songs get added to key playlists, and users get in-depth information regarding data on their songs, like skip rates and user-to-streaming ratios. User-to-streaming ratios are hugely valuable data points to see which of your songs are actually reacting the best on Spotify, Apple, Amazon, and Google Play, because you get to see how many people listen to one more than once.

Let's say you had a thousand listeners interact with one of your songs, and the actual number of *streams* you have for that track is two thousand. That means you have a 1:2 streaming ratio for that song. To say it another way, for every one of your users that interacted with that song, they, on average, listened to the song twice. And that's not bad. Ideally, depending on the service, you really want to see a ratio of 1:3 at least—for every one user, that user is listening to your song approximately three times—a good starting point for the digital service providers and their algorithms to say "Knock, knock. Hey! Pay attention to this song—there are signs of a life here!"

With the AWAL app, there are so many ways to slice and dice the data. No doubt, other services provide tremendous access to data and have their own apps, but right now, AWAL is our personal top choice.

One thing that could make the service even better would be if AWAL offered the option to split payments, factor in payable producer royalty splits, and sort mechanical royalty payments due to others. As of this writing, you need to account and split up payments among yourselves. This is assuming you have multiple people on your project and you need to pay out separately to a producer, other songwriters, etc. If you're just uploading your own project, though, it's likely you may not need these tools, so the lack of this feature is not a biggie at all, considering the overall exceptional service.

AWAL has a great and robust synch-pitching team in key cities around the world. And being a Kobalt music publishing client since 2006 with my publishing company, Brill Building,[41] and an AWAL client since 2014 with We Are: The Guard, I can attest that their synch team is incredible. This means you could have a team of creative artist and account managers pitching your songs for film, television, ads, video games, trailers, and the like!

Lastly, AWAL has one of the best technology platforms out there, hands down. It's all powered by Kobalt Music,[42] the parent owner of AWAL. They literally have a swarm of engineers and software coders continually making AWAL the best platform.

The icing on the cake is the personal service. Because AWAL doesn't take just anybody, you can be sure it means a lot when AWAL's creative managers tell their Apple or Spotify colleague they have the next big artist. AWAL is an excellent choice for a digital service provider, provided you can get in. Seeing as how it's free to submit, it can't hurt to try.

AWAL Review

Pros

- Streamlined app with actionable data
- Great analytics
- No upfront fees
- Pitching for editorial and playlists
- Label-like services for top artists
- Synchronization pitching
- Possible advances for top performers
- Partnered with YouTube's Content ID Program
- Hands-on support

Cons

- 15 percent commission, not a flat fee
- Not available to everybody
- No payment splitting/multi payable accounting services

TuneCore

TuneCore[43] is one of the original digital distributors on the market, and it seems it's a bit of a mixed bag, as far as the opinion of the internet goes.

Using TuneCore you can, just like all the other digital distribution services, submit your music to over 150 separate streaming platforms and stores without having to upload music to each one. TuneCore has access to all of the major streaming and download platforms, including Google Play, Amazon Music, YouTube, Apple Play, iTunes, and Spotify.

One of TuneCore's strengths, depending on how you look at it, is that they don't take any commission from your sales, so everything you make is yours to keep. That can be pretty amazing. For instance, if you have a song really taking off and it's garnering twenty million streams on Apple, that's going to be about $100,000! Yes!!

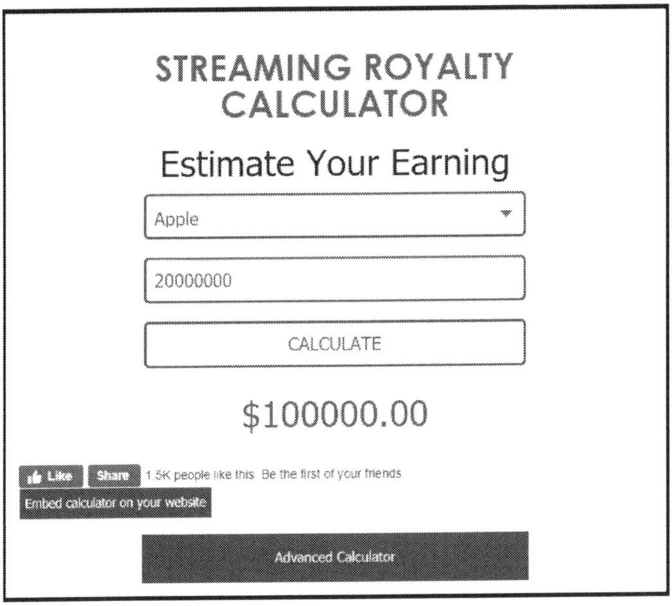

STREAMING ROYALTY CALCULATOR

Estimate Your Earning

Apple

20000000

CALCULATE

$100000.00

Like Share 1.5K people like this. Be the first of your friends

Embed calculator on your website

Advanced Calculator

One. Hundred. *thousand* dollars! Woohoo! How much does TuneCore take of that? Nada. Woohoo again! If you were with AWAL or another digital distributor that takes a percentage, your fee might be $15,000, which gets taken off the top before you're paid. Something to consider.

It works the other way too though. In truth, most songs that get uploaded to the DSPs have fewer than one to five thousand streams, so your chances of getting twenty million streams are extremely low. And TuneCore charges a yearly fee of around $30 for hosting your album for the first year. It costs $50 a year to continue to host your album for subsequent years. This can add up if you're hosting multiple albums via the service. In truth, it's probably a great model for TuneCore, as the majority of artists likely never achieve more than a few thousand streams per song.

One of TuneCore's other strengths is they really tout their synch services and pitching. Considering the power of a well-placed synchronization, that, along with no commissions, makes TuneCore worth a shot.

TuneCore Review

Pros

- Established company
- Access to over 150 streaming services
- No commissions
- Makes your music available for synchronization

Cons

- Annual hosting fees
- No payment splitting/multi accounting
- No additional support (as far as we can tell) for promotion, marketing, or playlisting
- Removal of your music if you cannot pay

DistroKid

Distrokid[44] is the newest of the DSPs, which is part of their appeal. Their interface is clean and easy to use. They don't charge any commissions, so you get to keep 100 percent of what you earn. There are fees, however, and some of the cool, neat-o features cost extra.

The most striking aspect of DistroKid is their alliance with Spotify and instant access to Spotify for Artists. Spotify has DistroKid listed as one of its most trusted digital service provider platforms. If you've been wondering how to get your music on Spotify, DistroKid is certainly a solid choice, but of course, it's not limited to just Spotify. DistroKid is partnered with over 150 streaming platforms. If you're looking to easily submit your music to as many of the popular streaming sites as possible, without having to manually upload music to each one, DistroKid could be a good option. But this is what everyone else basically does too.

You won't have to worry about your music disappearing when you use DistroKid. They offer a legacy program that ensures your music will stay online, no matter what. This makes them potentially a better pick than TuneCore, where you have to pay an annual fee to host your albums or they take down your music from stores. If you forget to update your credit card info, its removal can't be reversed and you have to start over.

DistroKid has its share of fees, but luckily they offer a variety of packages at varying price points, which I cover below. DistroKid is quite worth the price, considering all that they do.

Musician – This offers unlimited song and lyric uploads for one artist or band. It also lists your Spotify page as verified, so your fans will know everything on your channel is official.

Musician Plus – You can have up to two separate band or project pages, and you also get in-depth daily sales statistics, customizable URLs, scheduled release dates, preorder dates, and the ability to set prices on iTunes for downloads (depending if iTunes even exists by the time your reading this!).

Label Plan – You can manage between 5 to 100 artists on this plan while also getting all the benefits offered in Musician Plus.

DistroKid offers in-depth control over all of your online music. The YouTube Money feature is particularly useful. Like AWAL, DistroKid uploads your content to YouTube's Content ID database for a small additional fee. This monitors YouTube for other people using your music as user-generated content (UGC). If people re-upload your music to YouTube or, say, use it as the background music for their family vacation video, you'll receive the commissions instead of the uploader. They take a 20 percent commission whereas other DSPs offer the same service for free.

DistroKid Review

Pros

- No commissions
- Unlimited song upload
- No cost to sign up

- Extensive Spotify and iTunes/Apple Play features
- Email notifications when music goes live
- Support for numerous payment platforms
- Automated lyric uploads
- Music stays online forever (pending your plan)

Cons

- Some pressure to upsell services
- Shazam and Store Maximizer cost extra, while they're free for most other DSPs
- YouTube Money costs an annual fee plus a commission
- Basic analytics only with the Musician plan

CD Baby

CD Baby[45] is one of the oldest, most established digital service provider platforms out there. They have such an established online presence that they've built up quite an extensive catalog. There are over 300,000 artists signed up with CD Baby, with over 400,000 albums and an excess of three million songs. With so much content, you have a lot of people browsing. You just can't overlook the potential of a powerful, well-populated marketplace like CD Baby.

CD Baby also provides many of the functions that a traditional label would perform, such as keeping track of and collecting royalties. They bill themselves as kind of an anti-label, a leftover from the earliest days of music streaming.

With over fifteen years' experience in digital music, CD Baby has had time to get a number of things right in regards to helping musicians get their music out there, most notably, the customer support.

They're well-known for offering exceptional customer service for artists they represent, with all of that due to their exceptional founder, Derek Sivers,[46] who sold the company over a decade ago.

CD Baby Review

Pros

- No annual fees
- Physical distribution
- Store and fulfillment for vinyl and CDs
- Collects royalties
- Synch licensing

Cons

- A small charge for a single UPC/more for an album UPC
- No Instagram story music inclusion
- High YouTube commissions
- No payment splitting
- No marketing support

Stem

Stem[47] is one of the new kids on the block when it comes to digital service providers. If you're looking for a digital distributor for music with some of the most cutting-edge features mixed with traditional values like personal attention, quality, and ease of use, Stem will more than meet your needs. Stem was created with artists and musicians in mind, toward the goal of helping musicians make a living with their creativity.

For one thing, Stem offers artists the highest royalty rates of all of the digital distribution companies, and they offer playlist pitching to real playlist owners. Their back end has been a strong collaboration tool, making it quick, easy, and intuitive to split payments, share data, and manage contracts between multiple people.

You need to apply to be a part of Stem, and they are very particular about whom they bring on board. That's actually a good thing, as it ensures a certain level of quality is associated with the platform. It also means they're more able to offer personalized attention toward their.

Stem is particularly customizable, as it's some of the newest software created on the market. It allows for custom release schedules and strategies. You're able to differentiate different release dates for different platforms. You're able to see advanced data and metrics for each of those platforms as well, so you won't be left guessing how your promotions campaign is going.

Stem handles all of the regular duties that digital distribution services offer. Your music can be up and running on every major streaming platform in as few as five days.

Stem Review

Pros

- Among the highest splits paid to artists of approximately 10 percent
- Quality roster
- Many collaborative tools including splitting royalties and deep accounting
- PR Services
- Advanced data and metrics

Cons

- Earning requirements to be accepted
- High payment threshold
- No daily trend reports
- Inability to integrate with Instagram Stories

Human Re-Sources

Human Re-Sources[48] is a digital service provider from the son of Dr J (J. Erving). Julius Erving Jr has been working in the hip-hop industry for most of his life after a childhood surrounded by celebrities, no doubt thanks to his famous dad. Consequently, Irving helped broker a ton of deals and contracts for his clients, giving him a unique perspective into how music works, as well as some of its shortcomings. Irving believed that artists give away too much of their power to the record label. This is what he set out to remedy with Human Re-Sources, a digital service provider that also fulfills some of the functions traditionally fielded by the record labels.

Human Re-Sources' key claim to fame is that they don't charge a ton of fees. They only charge one minor distribution fee and otherwise stay out of their customer's way. The company is able to achieve this stripped-down approach by restricting their focus. They don't mess with physical sales or promotions in any way, instead focusing entirely on digital distribution. They also let their artists retain all of their rights, including ancillary revenue like merch sales and concert revenues. But none of the other services touch that either.

Human Re-Sources also offer some of the traditional advantages of labels. They reportedly handle promotions, help artists prepare videos and photoshoots, and offer marketing tools for social media and online platforms.

If you're looking for a no-muss, no-fuss DSP that offers top-shelf tools and resources without a lot of label interference, Human Re-Sources could be a good DSP company for you. To boot, there's more than just a rumor that Spotify is an investor in the digital service provider, so perhaps there's an additional plus in being associated with Human Re-Sources.... In fact,

> In an interview, Mr. Erving said Spotify had paid a modest advance that helped him establish his company. Human Re Sources, he said, is able to pitch songs directly to Spotify's internal teams—a rare advantage in the industry's vast do-it-yourself landscape.
>
> Spotify has not given favorable rates to artists affiliated with Human Re Sources, Mr. Erving said, and it has not guaranteed them placement on its playlists. But the company's artists have had success penetrating Spotify's most influential playlists, like New Music Fridays and Rap Caviar. Some of them, ... have also made it onto a Spotify billboard in Times Square.
>
> "Spotify has been very supportive of the stuff that we have released to date," Mr. Erving said. "But Apple and Pandora have been very supportive as well."
>
> – Ben Sisario, the *New York Times*[49]

With Spotify wanting to be neutral for all the artists out there, as well as many of the playlists letting algorithms and computer code and AI choose the songs for you more so than, say, those silly humans, we'll just have to see if this is an advantage.

Human Re-Sources Review

Pros

- Label services
- Only charge distribution fees
- Industry connections and clout
- Help with getting your songs in playlists and editorial features, especially via Spotify, apparently

Cons

- High fees of 20 percent (as quoted from The Source)

The Orchard

The Orchard[50] is another digital service provider that strikes a balance between being a music distribution company and a proper label, but they serve as more than just a digital record label, as they offer a number of digital distribution services, including video placement, to more than forty music markets around the world. They don't stop at online promotions either; they also help get their physical products and merchandise into their network of record stores, which are mostly located in North America and Europe.

The Orchard is what's known as a specialist aggregator, meaning they work with a highly curated clientele for a higher-than-usual 15 to 20 percent commission. Specialist aggregators tend to have much greater sway in the industry, as they're only working with top-tier talent. It's the DSP equivalent of being signed to a major label like RCA, Universal Music Group, Warner, or EMI. They also offer synch services, and being that synch services are normally a company in and of themselves, it's beyond useful that The Orchard offers the option as part of their services.

Their distribution services are powered by cutting-edge tech. Featuring slick templates for creating everything your music career could need to take off, from album covers to marketing materials. They also give you everything you need to help promote your content, including access to marketing professionals via their convenient app.

Finally, The Orchard lets you see how your content is performing with advanced analytics and detailed accounting. It takes the guesswork out of promoting your music, letting you know precisely what's working and what isn't.

The Orchard is an excellent choice if you're looking for something similar to a traditional record label but with all of the technological tools you need to help empower your music career. Your career could really flourish under their individualized attention, whether that's worth 15 to 20 percent of your overall revenue is up to you.

The Orchard Review

Pros

- Industry clout
- Global digital music distribution network
- Video placement
- Playlist placement
- Physical distribution
- One-on-one attention
- Advanced analytics and accounting

Cons

- Exclusive
- High commission

There you have it! While there are all kinds of new and existing digital distributors out there, at the end of the day, they all help get your music online so your fans and your future fans can listen and discover your music.

Handy-Dandy Comparison Chart

BENJAMINGROFF.COM
DIGITAL DISTRIBUTORS COMPARISON CHART

Name	Website	Sign Up Fee	Features	Commission	Analytics	Payment Splitting	Customer Support	Instagram Story Inclusion	Synch Liscensing	Open To All	Payment Threshold	Payouts
AWAL	awal.com	no upfront fee		15%	yes	no	yes	yes	yes	no	$45	n/a
TuneCore	tunecore.com	starting at $9.99 per single p/y		no	yes	no	yes	yes	yes	yes	none	Paypal, Direct Deposit, Mail
DistroKid	distrokid.com	no upfront fee		no	yes, but basic	yes (19.99 p/y)	yes	yes	no	yes	none	Various payment methods
CD Baby	cdbaby.com	starting at $19.99 p/y		9%	yes	no	yes	no	yes	yes	$10	n/a
Stem	stem.is	no upfront fee		10%	yes	yes	yes	no	no	no	$50	n/a
Human Re-Sources	human-re-sources.com	small distribution fee		n/a	yes	n/a	yes	n/a	n/a	no	n/a	n/a
The Orchard	theorchard.com	see commission fee		15% - 20%	yes	yes	yes	n/a	yes	no	n/a	n/a

Summary

The above companies will get your music uploaded and available to all the 150+ streaming services and downloading services. It's up to you, of course, to discover and get a feel for which service is the right fit for you. And if you happen to strike up a key personal relationship with any of these services, that might just be the icing on the cake.

More on that. I mean—look and let's be real. These companies *primarily* all do the same thing, which is—they get your music on all the streaming and download stores. Beyond this, it's really whether you're signing up on a percentage basis (15%) or a flat fee ala Tunecore. As important, if not most important, the other key thing is playlisting and editorial support. A lot of these services will *say* they're going to do this for you and pitch your songs to the editorial people at the DSPs—however, it's really going to be *your* job., Now—all things being equal, I would certainly almost always choose a digital distributor where there's ideally a personal relationship <u>*and*</u> someone who's SUPER passionate about my music. Why? On release day—you want to be with that person (and company) championing you and putting your music on the top of everyone's radar. This alone is worth way more than a 5% rate difference, say between comparing company "X" and company 'Y."

Disclaimer: This chapter is based on personal opinion and what my researchers and I were able to find online at the time, including researching each company's website. Of course, no results are guaranteed. Also, there's one thing for certain—things continually change. A year (or months) after this book is released, there surely will be new models, new companies, now offerings and different strategies. It's up to you as an artist, along with your team, to do your due diligence to find the right music release partner, but hopefully we have provided some helpful information to set your path in the right direction.

STEP 8

Develop Your Digital Marketing Plan

Advertising your music on
YouTube, Instagram, Facebook.

So you've uploaded your music to your chosen digital distribution service provider. Great. Now it's time to get your music in front of and actually heard by people. In other words, marketing, advertising, and promotion, baby! And just one of the people who can get the word out for you is a digital marketer. And this is probably going to be you, at least at first.

I know you're probably thinking at this point, *Damn, really? I thought my job was just to make music. And what the hell is a digital marketer?* In short, a digital marketer is someone who can take your assets (your music, videos, video snippets, banner ads) and set up ad campaigns across digital platforms to expose your music. This involves setting up a budget for ads and deciding how to effectively spend your ad budget across your social media accounts.

Fortune 500 companies, just like presidential candidates, use platforms like Facebook, Instagram, Google, and YouTube for their campaigns, but these ad networks are certainly also available to you too, even if you want to spend just $5 a day. For my own releases on We Are: The Guard, I use these digital advertising services all the time. In fact, our go-to digital marketing strategies usually include Google banner ads, Facebook and Instagram boosts and dark ads, occasional Snapchat and Spotify ads, and our favorite, YouTube.

Yes, YouTube. You know those pre-roll ads you see on YouTube? You can actually pay as low as one to three cents per view on YouTube to have your video seen in a highly targeted way, which is really the only way to be seen and heard when advertising.

Advertising on YouTube

Assuming you have a winning video, YouTube is probably my most favorite platform for advertising. For starters, you can really target who gets served your video, so you can choose potential new fans. Secondly, as mentioned, the costs to reach a potential new fan are so small. Especially for YouTube, the bang for your buck as it relates to digital marketing spend is fantastic, especially if you have an awesome, winning video. It's simply one of the best and most cost-effective ways to promote yourself. And if your video is so incredible that every person you pay to see the video forwards it to one or two other people, then you're going viral!

When it comes to YouTube, I can usually get our ad campaigns to about three cents or less per each targeted YouTube view. So let's say you have a female singer-songwriter, alt-pop artist project and you want to get the word out on your video via YouTube. You can target people in the United States, or even specific cities. For instance, if you want to expose people to your new release who are aged between eighteen to thirty-four; female; searching for Mazzy Star, Lana Del Rey, and Tori Amos; and who are in New York City and Los Angeles ... *kapow.* Done! If we really are competitive for our campaign and set them up correctly, we might be able to pay three cents a YouTube view. That means for an ad budget of just $500, you can reach about 16,750 people, and those views add up on your YouTube video. Ideally, we convert a percentage of those views to new fans who are also sharing the video and your music, thus amplifying and growing your true fan base, getting you to your thousand true fans mark even faster.

It is *crucial* to make sure your campaigns are set up correctly. Google, YouTube, and all the other advertising services provide so many ways to highly target exactly who you want to reach, so please take advantage of that. If you just set up a basic campaign to run your ad or show your video to whomever, you'll get taken advantage of by what some refer to as the Google tax for stupidity, and your ad spend will disappear very quickly. Everyone and anyone will be targeted to see your ad, including the eighty-year-old deaf grandmother living ten miles outside Chernobyl, and she was searching on YouTube for how to create fission out of radioactive snow.

Monitoring Your Results and Seeing What Works

Another important part of setting up digital marketing is monitoring the actions and cost per click, and the actions happening around your campaigns. For instance, you might find that doing an Instagram Story campaign might be a lot more effective than, say, boosting a Facebook post. Or that a YouTube campaign is really amplifying your music faster and in a more exponential way. By monitoring those metrics, you'll know where to shift your personal advertising spend.

There are so many books on this, and so many executives and consultants whose sole expertise is focused on how to run and set up these campaigns. For that reason, I'm just going to touch on this subject because

a) things change incredibly fast, and
b) there are people who can teach you how to do this way better than I ever could, and
c) there are people you can actually hire to do the work for you.

Instagram Story Ads

I think a tremendous online course on the subject is from an excellent music blogger called Ari of Ari's Take. In his course called *Streaming and Instagram Growth,*[51] Ari shows you how to set up your Instagram campaigns step by step, with a major focus on growing your followers and streams on Spotify through Instagram story ads. This course is not cheap, but I think it's invaluable. If you don't have the cash to plop down, maybe you and a few artist friends can each chip in $200 or so and share the costs. Just a thought. It's worth it to learn and use what he shares as a key part of your strategy in growing your audience on Spotify. The takeaway of the course is basically this—set up Instagram Story ads with a video / snippet of your music, which ultimately brings people to your Spotify Profile. On your Spotify profile, the user can listen to more music and/or ideally—follow you!

A key takeaway of Ari's course is that yes, it's great to have your song show up in Spotify's New Music Friday, but the *best* Spotify playlist to be on is basically your own Release Radar! This means that anyone who follows you on Spotify will get your song instantly added to the person's personal Spotify Release Radar playlist. The more real and credible followers you can obtain, the more credible streams you're going to have, especially on the first week of release. And that all helps your overall growth and maybe even the Spotify algorithm, assuming you have real fans "digesting," replaying, sharing and playlisting your music organically.

Hiring a Digital Marketer—Or Not!

If you can afford it, you can hire a digital marketer—you know, so it doesn't have to be you doing all this work and setting up ad campaigns. For a while, we were outsourcing all this work and paying $500 a month for a consultant to take care of our entire label for all our artists, which actually isn't a bad price. But we found, after taking Ari's course that I previously mentioned, that it didn't take a genius to set up these campaigns. That being said, there are people who make their living just setting up Instagram, Facebook, Snapchat, and YouTube campaigns; and they always have some tricks up their sleeves. They're also usually always on top of new trends, which makes them worth paying, and it takes the burden off your plate. Some things to think about, for sure, especially if you can pay a consultant a few hundred dollars a month to set these up for you.

Tip: Be sure to visit chapter 8 on outsourcing, where I talk more about platforms where you can find these people.

But if you can't afford someone right now, I simply recommend some YouTube and Google searches on the current best practices for setting up ad campaigns for each service. As mentioned, things literally change month by month, and there are always new services and new ways of doing things. It's going to be your job, especially in the beginning, to figure out the best way to promote your music and the best digital advertising platforms to get your word out on. Afterall, you've spent countless hours in the studio making your great songs, and perhaps also a video. Now it's time to actually make sure your art gets in front of people with some advertising spend.

Spending Money on Ads Is Not Cheesy.

Surprisingly or not, a few artists I've worked with over the years have expressed their view that advertising is cheesy. They don't necessarily want their music coming up and being viewed as ads to other people. I look at it this way. If a tree falls in a forest and no one is there to hear it, does it make a sound? It's the same way with your music. Additionally, while it might not seem cool to pay money for advertising, you don't think a band like Radiohead spends money on digital marketing?

It kills me sometimes to see artists who have a great song and a great video but fewer than a thousand views or streams. Just for a little ad spend, they could absolutely amplify their art to the right people who might not only be interested, but who might also become a true fan and help spread the word.

A Quick Word on Publicists—To Be or Not to Be?

Now often, when talking about digital marketers—the topic of publicists come up. Specifically, *should we hire one or not?* Now, let me tell you. I have a love-hate relationship with publicists—I've had great results but most of the time it's been—meh. Publicists, also known as PR people, are usually part of a marketing rollout. They have relationships with bloggers and media outlets. They service your music with a goal of getting a nice write-up in magazines and blogs like *Pitchfork, Pigeons & Planes, Rolling Stone, Billboard, New York Times,* or *Hilly Dilly.* But I'm going to be honest: If you're just starting out with your first releases, hiring those people right now is likely just a waste of money. As Ryan Holliday wrote in *Perennial Seller,* you're better off taking your PR fund in cash, setting it on fire, and posting the video on Instagram with the caption, "This was our PR fund." I think Ryan actually did this, which was a brilliant attention-getting tactic. But read my full opinion on hiring a publicist in chapter 13. Sometimes they can be great.

Here's what I ultimately found though, after throwing tens of thousands of dollars out the window. So, listen up! If you're just an artist with a song, EP, album—and a press release with a "one sheet"—asking "pretty please, write me up." It's likely no one will care. Remember, there are tens of thousands of artists also looking for a blog write up. Where publicists work the best, in my experience—is when you bring them a layup. And what's a layup? A layup is—you've basically done all the work for them—and the product (the artist) sells themselves. And voila—here are the key elements I find that are super crucial, especially if you want PR to do their jobs for you.

1. A cultural movement of some type. It could be something you stand for, from a stand point on sexuality, to politics to a new music movement or sub-genre. This is worth writing up about!

2. An artist who's highly visual and has a great visual identity and that those blogs and media outlets are going to want to have come in for an exclusive photo shoot (Hint: yeah, it's just not about the music. If you don't have a visual identity—let alone a sonic identity—now's the time to figure that out!).

3. Do you have a story to tell? Maybe you were, I don't know, raised by wolves or maybe you moved to the United States seeking political asylum? Or in the case of an artist I worked with, Jesse Saint John, he had a really great story. Jesse had previously written a slew of songs and hits for other famous artists such as: Britney Spears, Lizzo, Charli XCX, etc. and now Jesse was releasing his own music for the first time. It's his turn! In other words—there's something interesting and a story, above and beyond just the music that's interesting for the publicist to "sell" to the media outlet.

4. One other note. If your putting out a single and it's a cover record or a remix—generally, I would stay away from hiring a PR person. Those types of songs are generally more difficult to get blog "pick up." You can get some decent write ups—but really, you're swimming against the tide, as there's generally a lack of interest in my experience.

This is versus an artist who a publicist might be working who just has a "pretty cool song" and a boring one sheet. You now get the difference hopefully.

Summary

Digital marketing is crucial to help get the word out on your great music, and preferably also your great video. Assuming you've made a great song, EP, or album with a great video, it's no time to stop yourself short and let your music fall into a vacuum. It's time to promote it!

I know there's a lot information being presented in this book—and we're only a fraction of the way in! This is just a note that I have an amazing digital course called "Digital Release Blueprint—Music Marketing Strategies." In the course, I'll show you exactly what to do when—starting 6 weeks from your release date. There are over 70 video modules (!) and over 10 hours of content, where I show you exactly how and what to do week by week up to days before the release, the release day and post marketing release activities. Just visit my website at www.BenjaminGroff.com and you can find all the information there on the digital course. I'll be taking you personally (through the course) through each step of the release process—as well as multiple modules and over 3 hours of content on how to set up your Facebook, Instagram and YouTube video ads!

STEP 9

Submit Your Music

How to Submit Your Music to Submit Hub, EDM District, and Fluence.io.

For our artist releases at my label, We Are: The Guard, sometimes we'll hire a publicist—and yeah, as mentioned previously...sometimes we won't. Regardless, we'll always submit our new releases to these 3 websites / communities: SubmitHub.com, EDM District and Fluence.io. Let me tell you more about each.

SubmitHub

Instead of paying a publicist $1,000–$3,000 to send your songs to blogs and media outlets, you can spend just $50–$150 and buy credits at SubmitHub.com—where bloggers in their network listen to your song. For a little extra cash, you can make sure it gets a guaranteed listen. Simply load up your SubmitHub account with some dollars to buy credits. Then you can submit your song or video to any of the blogs associated and registered with the platform, which includes most of the key blogs. You should do your due diligence, though, and carefully select the correct genre(s) so your submissions are relevant to whom you're submitting to.

Now, I'm sure you're asking how effective this is? Well, sometimes the results can be zero, or maybe you'll get some mild blog pickup. Keep in mind you're literally sharing your songs with both some of the biggest blogs in the world as well as the bedroom blogger with a new WordPress and an opinion. However, I am excited to tell you that in rare instances, SubmitHub can be a home run. Let me give you an example.

Number one on Hype Machine for $200? Yes, I had that experience. My label, We Are: The Guard released a single on our label—and simply by using Hype Machine and the EDM District, we went all the way to number one on the Hype Machine[52] charts, all accomplished for $200, without using any type of PR or digital marketing—a huge return on investment. (The Hype Machine is a data-driven website that charts, in real time, the popularity of songs getting written up across the blogosphere.) In comparison, for that previous artist's release, we spent $1,500 for a publicist and they got us three lame blog write-ups.

The truth is, you never really know what's going to work. At the time of this writing, that song we had a big #1 on Hype Machine, has over 2 million+ Spotify streams and two juicy synchronization licenses, so I'd say that's a win! Alternatively, we've also had SubmitHub campaigns where we just get little or no pickup. It could be the song just wasn't as good as we thought, or maybe the artist wasn't cool enough for those snobby bloggers, or it didn't resonate. Or maybe there wasn't enough of a story. It's not the bloggers' fault. Part of doing this is knowing to be prepared for both success and some big whatevers. That in itself is a big life lesson. It's part of the game.

As a quick mindset tangent: If you put out your first releases and you see that stream count fall within that dreadful "<thousand" mark on Spotify, don't get down on yourself. It's part of the process in building your fan base. It takes time. Think of it this way. You might be at the 500-stream mark and maybe the next week you go up 50 streams more. That, my friend, is a 10 percent increase! It still feels like a zero though, right? Well, what happens when you have five million streams and go up 10 percent? Yeah, that's 5.5 million streams the next week and about $2,000 bucks in your pocket. And then things just go exponential.

A takeaway here is that it just never happens as fast as you want it to. The key is quality and consistency. Many of the biggest music icons in the world didn't really break until their fourth album, i.e., 40+ song releases over five to ten years! So, keep some perspective. All this stuff doesn't happen overnight.

EDM District

As mentioned before, if your release is more of an EDM / dance / electronic or remix track, or a chill-based song—you should definitely submit to EDM District. EDM District is a great company with the lock on those genres (EDM and chill) of YouTube curated channels, such as MrSuicideSheep or Majestic Casual to literally a hundred more. You'll have to sign a waiver allowing those YouTube channels to monetize your content on YouTube, but it's 100 percent worth it, in my opinion.

Fluence.io

Another service to closely monitor at the time of the writing of this book is Fluence.io. They may change their company name and web URL in the future, but it's another site I love, and I actually think it's going to be huge. It's the brainchild of the cofounder of TopSpin.

Fluence.io is similar to SubmitHub in that you're simply paying for someone's time to hear and review your music; however, the level of curators on the website is quite diverse, including a KCRW DJ and other A&R people, and myself.

Reviews are based on an hourly rate, and while it might look expensive at first—my hourly rate is $250[53]—you're only paying for their time to listen to your music. So, if you have a four-minute song, it might only cost you $15 to get a curator or an expert to hear it! You'll usually get some insightful feedback, and as a bonus, a percentage of those submissions have actually made it to our We Are: The Guard playlist and blog write-ups. And no shiz, wouldn't you know, we've also put out label and publishing offers on artists we've discovered through Fluence!

Ultimately, I think every meaningful curator is going to be (or should be) on this site, and I could see Fluence cutting out the publicist to be the middleperson between content creators and key media outlets and blogs. But let's see what happens.

Summary

In my opinion, when you're at the beginning of your career and just starting to create your story and foundation, why pay a publicist a wazoo of cash out your butt, when you can use SubmitHub, EDM District, and Fluence.io to get your music heard, reviewed, and potentially written up and supported?! Now, of course, if your music resonates and satisfies that "publicist checklist" as previously mentioned in Step 8—then, maybe it's time to hire a publicist, *and* you can *also* submit your music via these companies as well! Leave no stone unturned if you can.

STEP 10

Get Your Music in Movies, TV Shows, and Ads

$$$

This is a big one and can really move the needle for you—not just financially, but also for the overall exposure to your music. Consequently, you can bet this is also a great chapter in attracting your first thousand true fans. Your favorite nouns as an artist and writer are: synchs and synchronizations.

As I've mentioned before, synchronization licenses are all about your music getting placed in movies, movie trailers, television shows, advertisements, video games, apps, and more. For a little further explanation, whenever you see a moving image with music playing behind it, there's a synch license involved.

Controlling Both Sides (Master and Publishing)

There are usually two licenses that take place. If someone wants to license your music for a synch placement, they need to license both the publishing—whoever wrote the song, as well as the master—whoever owns the recording. It could be very likely that you, or you and your producer or band, own or co-own both the publishing *and* the master, so you get paid twice! If you record a cover record, you'll only be owning and controlling the master in this equation.

Synchronization licenses! Hell, yeah! Sign me up. How do I get this happening now!? It basically comes down to film/TV executives, music supervisors, and agencies and consultants having the close-knit relationships needed. Hopefully you can strike up relationships with these people throughout your career. You can do your research and find out just who these music supervisors are; however, if you can find a firm, consultant, or music publisher who can pitch your music to these music supervisors and executives, they're worth their weight in gold. And hopefully they can work on a commission basis and not on a monthly consultant fee basis.

Not only could you receive a great licensing fee, but once a synch is out in the marketplace—in a television spot or an internet advertisement—that synch literally has the potential to reach millions of people. You can bet a good handful of those will be shazaming and digging in the online forums to find the name of the artist and the song. For instance, have you ever looked up which new artist was used in the latest Apple commercial?

What's It Worth?

This is another very excellent part to a synch placement. A synch fee can be about $500 for use on a reality TV show, $1,500–$15,000 for a scripted TV show, $15,000–$30,000 for a movie trailer, $5,000–$75,000+ for use in a movie, and potentially a gazillion dollars if used in a big advertising spot. We're talking $500,000 for something that's Superbowl level. These are all just ballpark figures. It all depends on the cache of the brand, their budget, how they want to use your song, the territories or countries involved, the length of the license, the types of media involved, etc. It might not be any surprise that the more broadly a brand, TV show, or film wants to use your song, the more they need to pay up.

Synchs—How to Get 'Em

This all sounds great! But just how do I get that synchronization money and exposure? As mentioned before, it's about finding the right people who can represent you and who already have those great relationships in place. It's a much more trusted avenue than a cold pitch. And assuming you can find those people, you want to have time and logistics working on your side. Personally, I currently rely on my excellent administrator, Kobalt Music Publishing, for all my synch needs, and they kill it. They have a global synch team pitching my catalog all day long.

Timing

When it comes to releasing your music, you generally want to make sure that music supervisors are serviced your music through a trusted third party one to three months before it's actually released. And by servicing, I mean that your trusted source has sent these god-like and goddess-like music supervisors your music. Music supervisors are always dealing with future projects, so get them your music early enough to be fresh by the time the actual TV show or movie is released. Additionally, music supervisors are credible tastemakers as well. You can bet it's a feather in their credibility cap if they're the first to place this new awesome artist, aka you, before your music was known to the world.

One-Stop Shops

Music supervisors love these. I've found that you can have exponentially more wins when you can own and/or control both your masters and your publishing, so you can clear both sides of these at the same time with one call. They call these situations one stops.

Music supervisors don't want to work out puzzles and be labored with having to call, license, and get permission from three different writers on the same song with three different publishers, and then get permission for the master on top of that. So if you, or you collectively as the band, can give just one yes for the entire piece of music, that is incredibly important. Or it could be that maybe you are represented both on the master and publishing side by the same company, such as Kobalt Music Publishing (for publishing) and AWAL, Kobalt's digital label (for the master). If that's the case, then that qualifies as well, and getting your music cleared with one yes really can help make a difference.

Let me give you an example. Sometimes a studio needs to wrap on a Friday, and they need to finish clearing all the songs by the end of the day. This is where having full control over masters and publishing certainly helps. Just one yes is all the music supervisor needs to lock your song in place for the synch use. Compare this easy, one yes to a song that has five songwriters with five different publishers, and no one is sure exactly who owns the master. Now for sure, that last example might be clearable at some point, but to the music supervisor who needs a full clearance in the next hour, fuhgeddaboudit!

Synch Agencies and DIY Synchs

I'm going to give you some additional references and agencies who can help find these placements for you. Some of these are what the industry calls micro-synch agencies. Here's how it works. If you own or control both the master and publishing, you can upload to these platforms and be part of their ecosystem and synch libraries. These libraries usually always have amazing, robust search features for businesses who want to potentially license your music.

As an example, it's highly likely the local carpet cleaning company in Richmond, Virginia, can't afford Coldplay for their local TV ad, but maybe they can afford $500 to use your song that sounds like Coldplay. Or maybe it's an indie film and they only have $2,500 for their entire music budget. You can be sure that a lot of indie film directors are looking for great music on these sites. These sites are ever changing, but at the time of this writing, a few of the great ones are Music Bed, Marmoset Music, and Pump Audio (which is owned by Getty). Often, these services are nonexclusive, so if I were you, I'd sign up for all of them.

Contacting Music Supervisors Directly

If you can find some direct contacts for music supervisors, that's potentially great too. I say potentially. Keep in mind their inboxes will be jammed with unsolicited emails that often go right in the trash. I know this because I get pitched and solicited all the time as well. So when it comes to pitching, here's a piece of advice: if your music is amazing and original and creative, your emails should be too. Whenever I receive an email from a new artist which comes off as boring, unthoughtful, or generally lame, then I assume it's probably also going to be boring, unthoughtful, and lame music. Sorry, but it's my truth.

I've been doing this for more than twenty-five years. My expertise is not pitching for synchs and keeping up to date on all the briefs and shows that are out there. Nope. That's a full-time job for someone else who has equivalently done that type of work for ten or twenty years. Those are the people I want on my team so I'm not trying to do everything myself. You should strive to do the same. That's not to say you can't strike up a great relationship with a music supervisor and get placements, but either way, I'm giving you a bonus you can use for any pitching situation. Check out chapter 7 and 12 for my best tips on cold email pitching, including getting your emails opened, your links clicked, as well as the most common mistakes made in pitching your music. Additionally, in the Bonus chapter, I give you the links to the recommended resources and directories to find these film/movie and TV people.

Summary

Synchronizations can be an amazing opportunity to both

a) put some nice moolah in your bank account, and

b) get your music exposed to potentially millions of people, many of whom may add themselves to your first thousand+ true fan balance.

On top of that, a great synch can also add to your credibility. It's something you can certainly hype and tag on your one-sheet. And that one-sheet will certainly be a valuable tool you'll be using throughout your career. (Read more on the one-sheet in chapter 12).

STEP 11

Play Amazing Live Shows

Like, all the time!

Duh? Yes. When it comes to live shows, it's often where artists sell themselves short or just do the bare minimum (and hmm...maybe they don't know they're doing the bare minimum)? You see, most artists and bands can play competent shows, but they're usually far from amazing or original. Often, I'll leave a show thinking *You know, I could have watched that entire performance on YouTube and it would have had basically the same effect.*[54] This is one of the lamest things you can do for your audience. The best live artists not only play amazingly well, but they also put on a *real* show. Compare that to the 95 percent who don't. Oh, you played (and you didn't make any noticeable mistakes)? So what?

Why not be part of the 5 percent doing something totally different and unexpected. Make your shows a must-see. Make them *entertaining!* I hate to say it, but when you're out playing on a weekend night, you're not just competing with other bands performing that night. That's right. You're competing for attention against Netflix, Fortnite, the new superhero blockbuster film, Instagram, podcasts, virtual reality ... so you've got to make sure your live show is worth the trip and the ticket. You want to have the type of live show that a fan *needs* to get out of the house to see. It's a no-brainer.

At these shows, you never know what's going to happen or what to expect. These artists make their shows worth seeing. And while many of those artists may have some big costs on their production sets, someone like Peaches (who I'm proud to say I signed to Kobalt) sold out huge theatres with only a microphone and a 2-track CD of instrumentals in her early days. Peaches had, and continues to have, an amazing and original live set, compounded by her amazing originality and persona. You can also take someone like the artist Jewel, who, with just a guitar, can mesmerize an audience with amazing performances and equally amazing and sometimes hilarious stories in between.

You don't need a million dollars to put on a million-dollar live show. You just need some million-dollar original ideas and to put in the work to implement them like no one else.

What's the Identity of Your Live Show?

Think of it this way: If you're a modern contemporary artist and you're not selling sex, danger, your artist culture, high originality, revolution, or musicality at your live show, you might have a problem, because no one will care. Let me just quantify this. Motley Crue equates with sex and danger. Lady Gaga represents artist culture, sex, and some revolution. Bob Dylan's live show is about culture and revolution. Phish is about culture and amazing musicality. Rammstein and Gwar's live show is about danger. Going to see pianist, Glenn Gould (R.I.P.) play Moonlight Sonata 3rd Movement is about hyper musicality. You can and should incorporate and stand for something in your live show. Implementing *at least one* of those elements in your live show makes your live show a must-see, and one that gets written up in the local calendar section wherever you're playing next.

And also, to clarify—selling "sex" here—is not how it sounds. I'm not saying at all to "sell yourself" at all! More so—the concept of sexuality and live music has always intertwined. And that's not to say that your show needs to. Again—at all! As reference though and to clarify what I'm saying, looking back historically at Elvis or James Brown or Prince or Lady Gaga—sexuality, pushing the boundaries—has (and probably will always be) in vogue. Again, it doesn't mean at all that your show needs to. Your live show should, however, resonate what is absolutely *true* to you.

Lastly, having a great live show will not only convert potential fans to become part of your first thousand true fans, but it will likely put you over the top as far as finding anyone who's mildly interested in working with you. Let me give you an example. I recently made an offer to sign an artist. Upon experiencing her live show, I was totally blown away, and that never happens. I also realized that while my proposal was the first one in from the music industry, and I was still quite early in this artist's career, my proposal (in hindsight) didn't justify the level the artist is already heading toward. I told her after the show, "That was amazing! You know that proposal I just sent you? Let's just start over. After seeing you live, I realized that what you're doing is on a whole other level."

Just by seeing this artist's amazing live show, I knew instinctively that the word was not going to stay quiet for long, that the true fans were going to be ramping up, and the proverbial train would be shortly leaving the station. And as a label, I need to be on that train!

Summary

Your live show is crucial and cannot be just an afterthought. If you're showing up live to just play your music much like you do in your rehearsal space—with no show in your show—you're just not doing it right. I mean sure, you'll get by and people will applaud, but likely no one will be talking about or raving about you afterwards. A merely competent live show is simply not the path to really garner your true fans. Just like everything else in your career, you need to be doing something extraordinary live, something worth talking about.

Please read my blog post at BenjaminGroff.com, "Why Your Live Show Sucks, Part-1" for some epiphanies and ideas as far as elevating your live show.[55]

STEP 12

Grow Your Team

And have a written plan and assets ready for release day.

If or when things start taking off, you're going to want to start thinking about your team. This includes music publishers, agents, synch consultants, managers, digital marketers, artistic directors, publicists, attorneys, and maybe even that label. Every successful artist has an amazing team that's solely focused on building and supporting that artist, handling the day-to-day stuff, and leveraging their executive expertise so you can focus on your music expertise, making the best art you can. Fortunately, if you do this right, these executives and companies might actually start reaching out to you first (so make sure your social media pages are kept updated with contact information, and check those inboxes). Some of the best and most savvy managers, attorneys, and agents are also the best at finding new talent. If you've done your job right, *knock, knock!* Job well done.

When building your team, manage expectations—both yours and theirs. Essentially, you're doing yourself a favor by making sure everyone is on the same page with what you expect, and vice versa. Write it all down for future reference. Do this even before you start working together. I just know too many artists who got lured into a management situation or label/publishing deal who were promised the gates of heaven would open, to only later barely get their phone calls returned from same promisers. Or maybe they assumed that a manager was going to push their music to Spotify and Apple playlists, but the manager never had that intention. It's always good to be clear up front.

Sometimes a trial period might be a good way to start, or to have some written goals of what you're expecting in six- or twelve-months' time to make sure everyone is on the same wavelength.

A Written Plan

Boring? Maybe. Essential? Yes! Talking about your written release plan is not as exciting and cool as talking about making music, your video, standing out in a crowd, or your live show, but you want to have a written plan, especially when it comes to your releases. You're actually going to have to grab a coffee or three somewhere where you won't be interrupted, and really think and plan on how you are going to accomplish everything—when you're going to do things and who's going to do what.

When it comes to release day, you're going to want to have all your assets ready way in advance, assets meaning the music, the artwork, the social images, small clips, lyric videos, videos, memes, behind-the-scenes videos—basically a big folder of stuff that you can constantly use to promote your release. Trust me, there's nothing as stressful as waking up on release day and catching the falling knives of things you forgot to set up and/or create with no time left. So make sure you have your assets all squared away and have a plan.

As I've said before, as far as setting up your release, you'll want to upload to your digital distributor—like AWAL or TuneCore—four to five weeks before the release date. That will give you and the distributors plenty of time and a rampway up to the release. This is also important if there are any issues with the assets, which does happen, e.g., a wrong art color format or something that's not to spec. Pending your distributor, this also provides enough upfront time for them to pitch for playlists and market the music along with you.

Release Plan and Management Systems

When I say have a plan, I mean to also use a project management system. At my label, We Are: The Guard, we use Trello. Some people use Asana or just a big whiteboard, but for us, Trello works awesomely. It's basically a shared online productivity tool, where you can create actions and tasks based on cards. Imagine a huge wall of Post-its or filing cards. You can virtually move them around in different categories and also assign them to people on your team with due dates, attachments, and links.

When it comes to Trello and the release plan for my label, we have columns of cards (tasks). Each column has a time frame labeled. For instance, we have our first column titled "5–6 Weeks Before Release." Under this column are all the things that need to get done that week. We then have another column titled "3 Weeks Before Release," and so on, all the way up to "Release Day," and "Post Release" activities. All in all, I would say we have 75–100 tasks, pending the type of release, of different actionable cards that need to be handled for a successful rollout.

For each card, I have a step-by-step, no-brainer process on what needs to get done, including directions, technical specifications, email scripts, and also who to get in touch with, how something needs to get done, etc. It's essentially a paint-by-numbers and time-tested plan that I've built over the last five years, which has provided great results for the label—we've surpassed over one-hundred million cumulative Spotify streams as I'm writing this! You can actually get a free download of what I call the Release Blueprint PDF plan at BenjaminGroff.com/Release.

And actually, great news for you—this "Release Blueprint" I've actually turned into an entire digital course! The course contains over 70 video modules and over 10 hours of content, where I'm personally taking you through each task and activity, explaining in full detail—what to do when and how to do it. From 5–6 weeks before your release, all the way up to the release day and post release activities. Check it out at BenjaminGroff.com and look for the "Courses"—you're going to get the exact release plan that I've created for my label!

WE ARE: THE GUARD - RELEASE BLUEPRINT

(Bonus Content from "~~HOW DO I GET A RECORD DEAL?~~ SIGN YOURSELF!")

5-6 WEEKS BEFORE RELEASE

- Reference Links
- Giving Yourself the Gift of Time (Solving Digital Delivery Issues)
- Create and Compile Your Folder of Stuff (Jpegs, behind the scenes, day in the life, studio sessions, photos, etc)
- Lets Upload a Single Pt 1 - Compiling Assets
- Let's Upload a Single! (Digital Upload Process from Start to Finish)
- Uploading an EP or Album (with or without Pre Existing Tracks)
- PR Publicity - Who They Are When to Hire - My Love Hate Relationship (Consider Hiring a PR Person + My Love & Hate Relationship With Them)
- Filling out the AWAL - Digital Distributor Pitch Form (Filling Out the AWAL Pitch Form (Audio) - Provide Supporting Material & Excitement to Your Digital Distributor)
- Synch Dept Servicing - Including Publishers and Cowriters Publishers
- Create a Written Marketing Plan (Create Marketing Plan-to be shared internally and with management/artist)
- Find a Gig to Play on Release Day (Start looking for a gig to perform on Release Day or Release Party/Event)
- Brainstorm Possible Non Traditional Events

4 WEEKS BEFORE RELEASE

- Submit and Claim Your Spotify and Apple Profile (Submit and Claim Your Spotify and Apple Artist Profile (as well as Pandora and all other digital service providers)
- Get Spotify URI & URL and Apple URL from Digital Distributor (Get Spotify URI / URL and Apple URL (once ingested) from Digital Distributor)
- Share Spotify & Apple URI - URL with Team (Share Spotify & Apple URI / URL with artist / artist management for any playlisting or promotion they want to do on their end.)
- Upload Your Music to Micro Synch Agencies (Sign up and Upload Your Music to Micro Synch Agencies)
- Touch Base with Global Distribution Offices (Touch base with Digital Distributor Offices & Synch Teams & Other Parts of Your Team - London, Stockholm, Berlin, Sydney, etc.)
- Review Best Practices - Spotify, YouTube, Apple, etc. and make necessary changes
- Review 50 Ways to Promote a Single by Jake Udell (Review 50 Ways to Promote A Single by Jake Udell / Art of a Manager)
- Setting Up Google Alerts (Make sure you have Google Alerts Set Up)

3 WEEKS BEFORE RELEASE

- Pitch on Spotify Artist Deck / DSP Playlisting
- Get Key Video Clips - Assets Made (Get Key Video Clips, Gifs, Memes, Photos, Behind the Scenes, PR photos, Life in the Day Of, at the Studio made and stockpiled)
- Get a One Sheet Made or Updated
- Wavo Introduction and Consideration (Wavo.Me - look at promoting through the Wavo Network)
- PR - Publicist Should be Shopping a Premiere (Plus Why Release on Tuesday or Wednesday)
- Pitch Songs to EDM District (YouTube Distribution & Curation Channels) (Submit Music to EDM District and their Amazing Network of YouTube Channels)
- Commission a Lyric Video (Get a Lyric Video Commissioned + Outsourcing Video Content / Strategies)
- Consider Hiring a Digital Marketer or Digital Freelancer

2 WEEKS BEFORE RELEASE

- Create Social Media Skins for Your Release (and Maybe Google Banner Ads) (Get Google Ads and Social Banners Made or Create Them Yourself)
- 101 Primer on Google Ad Network, YouTube, Dropping Pixels, Audiences, Remarketing
- Research and Submit - UGC Spotify Playlisting (Start Researching Spotify UGC Playlists)
- Get music to Blog Friends for their support and playlisting
- Figure out Instagram - video clips under .60 seconds and what that will be and make edit
- If You Have DSP Contacts i.e. Spotify, Apple, Amazon, Tidal etc. Remind them about the Release
- Instagram Clips made - Strategy Sorted
- Get a Pre Save Email Campaign Ready
- TikTok - Utilizing Influencers and Challenges (Consider an Instagram or TikTok Influencer Campaign (Using UpFluence or other Campaign Management System)

WE ARE: THE GUARD - RELEASE BLUEPRINT

(Bonus Content from "~~HOW DO I GET A RECORD DEAL?~~ SIGN YOURSELF!")

1 WEEK BEFORE RELEASE

- Video Assets we are going to use should be Delivered this Week and put into the appropriate folders.
- Have an Approved Press Release (aka Your Presser) (Have approved "Presser" / Press Release from PR firm)
- Media Outlet for Premier - Locked In
- Prime Influencers and Connectors in helping with the push
- Alert Your Network About Your Release (Artist Friends, Blogs, Supporters)
- Work Artist playlists / reciprocal playlisting
- Post and Run a Pre-Save and Pre-Add Campaign
- Linktree 101 for Instragram (Update LinkTree with Pre Save etc)
- Confirm Who Is Doing What with Your Team!

2 DAYS BEFORE RELEASE

- Upload Files to Soundcloud (Plus Pro Tips) (Upload assets to Soundcloud (private) and give description and links for artist)
- Confirm, Proof and Green Light the Press Release / Presser

1 DAY BEFORE RELEASE

- Upload Video Assets to YouTube (Plus Pro Tips) (Upload Assets to YouTube (private) and give description and links)
- Make sure the song / album did get uploaded correctly - check at 9pm PST
- Rally Connections between Friends and Celebrities to share the song
- Prepare Emails for UGC Playlists
- What can you give away Free for an Email / Collecting Fan Emails or Cell #s
- Upload to Audius - What Is Audius and Why You Should Care (Consider Uploading to Audius.co)

DAY OF RELEASE

- Pandora AMP (Setting Up Free Ads and Messaging in Pandora)
- PR to go Live / Wide
- Submit Hub / Fluence.IO Go Live
- Take Social Media Campaigns Live
- Put up Banners on Social Channels
- Rally friends and fans to listen and share music (plus some other tricks)
- Make sure injested into Pandora
- Make sure everything is live - Soundcloud, YouTube, with Descriptions and Links
- Send out email blast for Fans!
- Adjust Artist Pick on Spotify and/or Trade off with another Artist reciprocal look
- Put Release in top of LinkTree on Instagram
- Facebook Events - David invited you to Breathless - New Single Release. Let David know if you can make it. Tell him you're going
- Setting Up a YouTube Video Campaign
- Send Emails out for UGC Playlisting

POST RELEASE - IDEAS

- 50 Post Release Marketing Ideas
- Consider Working "In Store" Radio Play
- Continue looking for Spotify ads and look for supporting evidence in streaming ratio. Need 2.0 or above for signs of life.
- Consider In2une www.in2unemusic.com - If signs of life for radio
- SoundExchange submission
- Reviewing Your Team and Seeing who you can add (or subtract) i.e. Managers, Lawyers, Publishers, PR for next Releases, etc.
- Post Release - Getting the PR Pickup Report (Get (or Create) a Report on Blog Pickup and Support)
- Post Marketing Release Review

Summary

The twelve steps are just really *part* of the journey. There's plenty more required for you to have a successful rollout plan, which I'll cover in the next chapters. Essentially, it's important to have it, meaning *your plan*, written down. This might take some time to accomplish, but I totally believe you'll find the exercise to be of tremendous benefit. The bonus is you can duplicate your written plan for each and every one of your releases. I've found time and time again that simply winging it doesn't work out too well. You'll probably inspire and come up with other ideas along the way.

12-STEP SUMMARY

You made it! You now know what it takes to acquire your first true thousand fans! While this is in no way an overnight process, you'll definitely have more than you did when you started your new journey. And are there plenty more steps you can and should be doing? Hell, yes! These are just my twelve bullet-point steps to getting the ball rolling. Each plan and course of action is going to be totally different for each artist.

And of course, the sole purpose here is attracting and cultivating your first thousand true fans. The additional benefit here is that if done right, we'll have the labels calling you rather than the other way around. In short, by the end of going through this process a few times, you'll have accomplished at minimum the following, as well as being wayyyy ahead of most artists on the same path.

1. Released amazing songs.
    - Created and produced amazing, original, must-listen-to songs and music product.
2. Clearly defined yourself as an artist.
    - Created and defined a signature sound. Identified who your tribe is, which also answers who you are as an artist.
3. Released quality music frequently.
    - Created social media pages where you continually provide fresh content with up-to-date contact information.
4. Defined your social media voice.
    - Created a signature digital voice for your socials.

5. Created winning videos.
    - Created exceptional, winning video content that might go viral.
6. Grew your fan base.
    - Given your music away, as well as personal experiences with you for free, with the goal of getting your first true thousand fans.
7. Got your music on the DSPs.
    - Determined and locked in your digital distribution partner.
8. Developed your marketing plan.
    - Created and set up a written, digital marketing plan.
9. Submitted your music to curators.
    - Uploaded your music on all digital platforms. Used submission services like Submit Hub, EDM District, and Fluence.io.
10. Got your music in movies, TV shows, and ads.
    - Found a synch consultant and had your music serviced to movie/TV supervisors, uploaded your music to micro-synch agencies.
11. Developed your unique live show performance style.
    - Created a live following by doing something totally different and original than everyone else.
12. Grew your team and set up a release day planning template.
    - Created a team of gurus and experts around you that can help accelerate your career.
    - Created a written plan you're going to follow that can be repeated again and again for each release.

If you've done this right, you'll have started a buzz and more importantly a real, true fan base, which is what all the indie and major record labels and music publishers are looking for. Like I said before, if you build it, and your stuff starts resonating, the labels will come.

Now, also remember, this is not a "once and done" process. If you've gone through the 12 steps with one of your releases, now it's "rinse and repeat" time. You can use this same process over and over. And why should it be you doing all this work? Let me remind you…

A&R People aka Swimming with Sharks

Like sharks, most record executives need to smell some blood in the water. Forgive the analogy, but sometimes you have to chum the waters to get their attention. Trust me, there's nothing more exciting to a label than an artist who has:

- a finished product,
- already garnered a few million streams collectively on the handful of first releases,
- releases that are starting to show up on Spotify algorithm reports, and
- live shows that are starting to sell out, even if they are in small, two-hundred-capacity rooms.

This is like crack cocaine to record labels.

Now that you've laid all the groundwork and have a business plan that works, the labels will seek you out and want to be in partnership with you. They'll likely want to buy into your business plan, aka your art and the artist culture you've built.

Note: The above numbers and metrics are not exactly what labels are looking for, but it's a good indication and ballpark of what you minimally want to shoot for. In other words, don't expect a label to be calling if you only have ten thousand streams on your last release, even though those numbers are a pretty good start. You need to just continue to do great work, be diligent, set up your records, regularly release consistently great music, and be amazing!

BONUS!

The We Are: The Guard Release Rollout Plan

As I mentioned, there are dozens, if not hundreds, of steps that could be involved in your breakthrough. I stuck to a 12-step program, though, as I felt those twelve steps were the most crucial to focus on and it helps with overall clarity. However, I want to give you more detail and context.

While I've been a music publisher for over twenty-five years, it's more recently, where I've come up with release plans for singles, EPs, and albums. My expensive education in this area (what I learned with my own money) is now at about the six-year mark. It all started when I released Mother Falcon's incredible music—a sixteen-piece symphonic indie band. Seriously, check them out![56] While our releases with Mother Falcon have all been in the green and profitable, there are other releases where ... how should I say it ... I made some expensive mistakes in my educational journey of releasing records. Look, I know that not every release is going to take off to the moon. Expensive lessons will be made in everyone's career, including yours, and we have to understand that this is part of the process. We're going to have our share of amazing wins and some that just don't work out. You and I can only do our very best at the end of the day.

That being said, I have something very special for you, which cost me about $50,000 of mistakes, and about a thousand hours of trial and error. As mentioned previously, you can get a *full* PDF cheat sheet of my release plan for *free at www.BenjaminGroff.com/Release.* Look at that—it appears I'm again taking some of my own advice and giving away this release plan PDF, which has tremendous value, for free! Well, in exchange for your email.

I really recommend you grab the PDF, print it out, view it on your computer or phone, and refer to it all the time.

You see—what I found happening in my earlier years of releasing records is I would only have "kind of" have a plan. Release day would sneak up, usually faster than we expected, and I'd be like, "Oh damn, I forgot to do this. Where's this video asset? Arrghh, we forget to set up XYZ!" And then we were running around catching falling knives. That's never a fun thing, especially when you have your artist's (and your own) career on the line. That's when I created our overall release plan in my team's shared Trello online management system.[57]

Compare that orderly rollout to what I think a lot of artists do, which is, "I want this song to come out next week for no reason. Which digital service can I use to get my song online the fastest? I'll just pick a random date two weeks away, upload to my DSP, and maybe announce the single on my socials, and that's it. That might work for some artists, but very few. What I've found is that you need a plan. This "Release Blueprint" PDF, which I'm offering for free, is the cumulative repository of all my release knowledge. This overall plan is for you to review and pick the best parts for your own release strategy.

As I've said, the free PDF is "the" We Are: The Guard release plan. The PDF may lead you to the proverbial water, or millions of streams, in this case. It's the exact plan my label has used to generate over one hundred million streams (just on Spotify), and it's my gift to you to visually see and understand how we're rolling out our singles, EPs, and albums so you can use it for your own releases.

The PDF is a small part of my in-depth digital course called The Release Blueprint. Read more about it at BenjaminGroff.com/Release and feel free to check out some the key previews.[58]

PART 3

SECRETS IN DOING IT

7

PUTTING LOVE, ENERGY, AND ORIGINALITY INTO MARKETING

Repeat after me: I'm not just going to "hand over" my marketing. It's my job.

If you've diligently read this book up to this page and paid attention, e.g., while not concurrently binge-watching your latest Netflix show, you've hopefully picked up some unique marketing ideas to build your email list of followers and also plumped up the awareness of your music across platforms, all in the name of acquiring your first true thousand fans.

The Ryan Holiday Effect—Putting Love into Marketing

So it's time to do a little mindset shift. Yes! It's time to banish the thought of marketing as someone else's boring job. We're going to try a new perspective that marketing is something you're actually looking forward to in a fresh and exciting way. I implore you to make this mentality change, along with someone who will likely change your life, Ryan Holiday.

Ryan Holiday is one of my favorite (and relatively new) authors. I always pick up major epiphanies from his books. The kind of inside joke here is that Ryan Holiday wrote *Perennial Seller* about literally making perennial sellers and in that process, you guessed it, ended up writing a perennial seller—a thing that just sells, sells, and sells all the time, year after year, even without promotion because it's just so darned good. This applies to film, literature, music, even food items on menus.

Comparatively, I believe we are in a musical era of fleeting songs that will not stand the test of time, much less get any attention at all, yet every year we have new songs that rise to the top and stand out. They have become part of our culture and will forever be on the radio and/or circulation in our playlists. I really believe these types of artists and songs are just fewer and fewer these days. I know because I'm always trying to find them 'em to sign them up. No doubt, a lot of the classics were created from the '60s, '70s, '80s, and '90s, but there's still an opportunity for you to create a perennial seller.

A favorite quote I heard from Billy Joel in person went something like this: "I'm merely a competent artist, vocalist, and songwriter. But in an era of incompetence, that makes me extraordinary" Billy Joel said that about twenty-five years ago. Today, the environment is *ripe* for an artist, aka you, to continually deliver perennial sellers—because the bar today is just so low.

Ryan Holiday maintains that once you make your great piece of work, your album, EP, single, book, etc., you just don't hand it over to someone else to do the marketing. Nope. In today's world, you are the marketer, and you have to come up with the marketing plan. This isn't just about how much you're going to spend on Facebook ads. It's about spending the same amount of love, originality, creativity, and passion in marketing and promoting your piece of work as you did in making your project.

Have a Story (and Music!) Worth Blogging About!

This is where it's time to get creative and maybe even a little proverbially dangerous and outside the box. Yes, it's time for you to take off that creative artist hat and instead switch it out for the creative marketing hat. And just like we applied a mindset of being unique and original and outside the box to making your art, we're going to put that same type of energy into marketing. In other words, if you're thinking that marketing idea is just too crazy, you might just be onto something.

Let me give you an example. As I mentioned earlier in the book, I'm really excited and proud to be working with an artist called MXMS.[59] Instantly, just visually seeing them or needle dropping two measures of their music, you should know what they're all about. They've done a great job with their identity, not that they had to work on it; it's simply who they are.

MXMS is a dark indie pop/goth pop/dark electronic artist. They've even created their own music genre, which they call funeral pop. I highly implore you create your own music genre, if you can.

MXMS came up with some nontraditional marketing ideas, one being calling their tour RIP x VIP: While the band is on tour and in your city, you can come meet and hang with the band in an actual cemetery and delight in some black cake and black coffee. They sell the RIP x VIP experience as an exclusive, limited package online, which helps support them while on tour.

Another idea I had for our next EP release is to have an actual funeral for them in a mortuary or funeral home. It would be a real event, with real guests, eulogies, etc., and essentially, they would be attending their own funerals in the caskets. As morbid as that sounds, we'd invite guest bloggers and media, and also film it as a mini documentary/experience for social media.

Make Them Care / Make It Easy

Those are just two examples, but they are radically different then writing a press release and doing a media blast that's just going into a thousand spam folders. You don't want to be that person with the lame strategy everyone else has. No. One. Cares. About your email. What they care about is your story, like an RIP x VIP experience. Media outlets and bloggers all need a story to tell. If you don't give them one, why should they care?

Emails

Compare these two different pitches and subject lines that could show up in a blogger's or media editor's inbox on a band I just made up called Gothic Toxic.

> **Subject:** _____________ (Artist Name) releases new EP "Mortuary." Listen Now.
>
> or

> **Subject:** ______________(Artist Name) holds their own Funeral at Shady Lawn Mortuary. Open for Post Mortem Listening Party Invite for New EP "Mortuary."

If you're a media outlet, blogger, or curator at a DSP, which one of those emails are you likely going to click through and read further? In fact—if you're a blogger you may "definitely" need to cover this event—and the music!

Summary

Marketing your music, especially in the beginning, and probably forever more, is going to be your job. Sure, ultimately, you'll be able to find someone to help set up all your digital marketing and ad spend, but for now it's going to be your job to come up with stunning new ways to stand out and be as original, creative, and compelling as your own artistic product.

8

FREE UP YOUR TIME

Hiring consultants, freelancers, and virtual assistants via UpWork, Creative Commissions, and Fivver

I have an important question to ask you. How much is your time worth? Really. In a perfect world, you'll eventually be hiring and outsourcing all that malarkey and BS stuff that

a) you don't want to do and
b) you can pay someone else to do for a lot less than your theoretical hourly rate.

All this freed-up time leaves you only doing the work that's in your unique ability—making great music and songs, working on your craft, perfecting live shows, and working on your creative marketing. Because this is your job now.

Value Your Time

Did you know that songwriters actually have the ability to perform work that can earn them one million per hour? Yes, some of the biggest songs ever were written in fifteen minutes or less. Think about that! Songwriters and Wall Street bankers have one thing in common—they both have the ability to earn ridiculous hourly rates! If you think of it this way, songwriters have one of the most profitable hourly professions in existence! So why, when you have the potential to make this kind of money per hour, would you instead spend hours

- trying to figure out how to make a lyric video,
- cropping some images in photoshop,
- trying to learn how to set up YouTube ads in Google AdWords,
- tuning and comping your vocals, or even
- setting up your own website and social media pages, much less managing them?

You get the idea. Of course, if you love doing that stuff, for sure continue to do your thing, but my bet is you hate all that crap. I hate it, but the good news is there are people out there you can hire, often on the cheap, who are not only experts but who actually *love* doing this stuff.

How to Find Your Army and Exponentiate Yourself

I'm happy to tell you that you can leverage and amplify yourself incredibly effectively in a various number of ways. One of them is a company called Upwork.

Upwork[60]

I use the service all the time, and I have for at least a decade, even when they were called oDesk. There's a global workforce on Upwork with a ton of people on it working from home. They've said goodbye to the corporate nine to five, and many of them are amazing rock stars at what they do. In many cases, they only charge a fraction of what other corporate companies would charge.

For example, I found a great guy in Estonia who, for $10 a song, will make stock videos for me that I can use to populate my YouTube channel. For $150 he'll make fantastic lyric videos, ones that usually would cost ten times that much to hire someone in Los Angeles. *I hope he's not reading this book; my rates will go higher.* Here's the kicker—this lyric video guy is so good that many of these lyric videos have each gone on to stream over one million views on YouTube, and a few over two million+! [61]

Virtually (no pun intended), you can find almost anyone to do anything on Upwork.com. My profile is on there too. [62] For now, I'm offering hourly coaching. You can hire me to listen and critique your songs and help with strategy with your artist career for an hourly rate. I'm not inexpensive, but I have to value my time, and you'll get your money's worth.

Upwork's freelancers can help leverage you until you become the boss and have an army of consultants, creative people, and virtual assistants helping you move the needle for your career.

Imagine if you could pay someone as little as $7.50 to $15 an hour to manage your social media accounts, help with the logistics of your tour, edit your videos, create banner ads, find qualified coders to create your webpage, create your artist logo, etc.! Basically, just like a major or indie record label, you can outsource all this stuff you don't want to do as an artist.

A lot of the lower cost, but still highly qualified, talents will be in the Philippines, India, Estonia, Pakistan, etc., so definitely expect somewhat of a language barrier. For many of these people, their language might be great or near perfect in emails and texts but not so great talking over the phone. That's fine. They're not running customer support for you or anything, but you do get what you pay for, and diligence is required on your end to screen the best people.

And on that note, you should really consider ponying up the bucks to hire the most qualified person you can. Overall, the lesson I've learned is it's cheaper to hire a $25 to $50 an hour person who is an expert, who can get something done right the first time, versus a $10 an hour person who will need more handholding and overseeing, and who often doesn't care as much about the work. It's up to you to vet everyone on your team.

Currently this is my small army team on Upwork:

- 4 music blog writers separately based in Glasgow, London, Phoenix, San Diego
- 1 general manager of our music blog based in San Diego
- 1 social media specialist in London
- 1 SEO guy in Berlin
- 1 video content creator (my Estonia guy)

Beyond those people, my webmaster is from my hometown in Pennsylvania. None of them come in to work at the office, and they all work on their own time. While I do have an office, I also have this virtual office.

The takeaway here is to leverage yourself and let someone else who's an expert in that field do the job for you. And not just do the job, but do it ten times better than you ever could at one-tenth of the typical corporate rate. Create a virtual team of these experts so you can focus on what counts, which is creating your music and solely working within your own unique ability.

Fiverr[63]

Fivver is another great company that's also within this new ecosystem the media is starting to call the "gig economy." Just like you may be able to request a private chauffeur to take you to your destination for $10—on app platforms like Uber and Lyft—Fivver is a marketplace supplying an army of freelancers who are ready to do any job for you for $5. Well, let's qualify that. It used to be any job for a $5 base rate plus different tiers. Today it seems more like it's any job in $5 increments. Fair enough. But I love Fivver.

As it pertains to yourself as an artist, there are categories here you might find useful: e.g., graphic design, digital marketing, video and animation, music and audio, and more. For instance, let's look inside the Music & Audio category. Ahh, here we go, vocal tuning. You may or may not have guessed, but one thing I hate doing is vocal tuning and comping. So, let's say you're an artist and you need to clean up, time align, and tune your own vocals. Or maybe you're a producer working with an artist and you need vocal cleanup help, and you're totally overloaded with deadlines. You could take four hours to do that vocal comp and tuning or you could spend a small $35 and have someone take care of that for you, thus freeing up time for you to do your million-dollar-an-hour work.

Or how about video animation—lyric videos? *Yes!* As you can see, with Fivver there's no need to learn kinetic typography and spend your incredibly valuable time to make a lyric video. For much less, that same video will be made by an expert. It might be your first lyric video you ever make. Do you really want a novice lyric video made by you to represent your great song? Also, you might do a great job, but how long is that going to take? My thought is why not hire an expert who loves to make lyric videos and has been doing it for years. Why not work smarter? Fivver even has whiteboard and explainer video creators. There are tons of services here that are geared toward helping you, the artist, by taking the heavy lifting off your hands.

One other idea: What if you put your own profile up here for some extra cash? Maybe you're a great guitar player or vocal arranger, and you don't mind freeing up four or five hours every week to lay down some tracks and record for other people. Having a profile on Fivver could be an income stream in achieving your first level of making it in the music business i.e., doing music full time!

In short, high five for Fivver!

Creative Commissions[64]

The Creative Commission marketplace usually requires a more robust budget, but it works along the same idea of Fivver; however, Creative Commissions is much more specific to video creation and video content.

The idea here is that you don't need $20,000 to make a great music video. Simply put, there are qualified people around the world who can create a video that looks like it was made for $20,000 but only costs $2,500.

Again, you need to do your due diligence here, but the idea is you'll post an exact brief for your music video with your music, and maybe a mood or visual board. Then amazing video directors, animators, and video creators from around the world will virtually submit treatments and bids to create your video.

Some of these video creators will be up-and-coming video directors; film students; hungry, great, creative people; firms looking to develop their work reels; or maybe even video creators who already have amazing video footage and need some great music to synch it to. Creative Commissions also has more high-end and experienced people who might demand upwards of the $5,000 to $10,000 scale and beyond, but their prices will probably be worth it.

Creative Commission is simply brilliant, and I know at least one fantastic indie label whose video content is primarily sourced from Creative Commissions.

Finding Quality Outsourcers

It's going to be very difficult conceptually, if not impossible—especially when you're on a budget—to get something done to 100 percent of your expectations. If you're getting the final product, or someone is doing a job for you, try to learn to be happy with 80 percent.

"Be satisfied with 80 percent of quality."

—Richard Branson (well, at least that's what I heard from someone that knows him)

Obviously 95 to 100 percent would be ideal, but maybe 80 percent of perfect is the best that can be done. Don't sweat it. Even if the work comes in at 70 or 80 percent of the quality you'd like, you can work with the person you've hired and punch it up to 95 + percent. Either way, it should be a net win for you as far as your time, final product, and effort is concerned.

Note: I do realize that for some people, this chapter might be a little out of reach as far as budgets go. Some of you might only have beer money at the end of the month to build these assets, but there are always creative ways to do things if you really want to get things done. You can consider trades and bartering. For instance, someone you know might be a great video animator and you might have a great song, or maybe you're a great musician. By working together, you might be able to collaborate. You could make a great track for their video and they then make a video for your song.

But wait, there's more! You know what's even better than someone taking as much off your plate as possible so you can do more important work? It's finding people who can free up *all* your time so you can do no work at all. That's right—take the day off! If you can find some great partners, maybe you could free up ten hours or more every week for *you.* Imagine what you could do with an extra ten hours a week: finally get some quality sleep, do something creatively nourishing, spend time with friends and family.... And those special moments can help cycle priceless energy and inspiration back into you and your music.

Summary

Why give up your valuable time for work that:

a) you really don't like doing,
b) you can't do well, or
c) someone else can do ten times better

Start working with the companies previously mentioned, or others, to free up your time to do the work that only you can do—writing and recording amazing songs.

Recognize what your time's worth. It's worth *a lot* more than you realize.

9

PITCHING YOUR MUSIC FOR UGC SPOTIFY PLAYLISTS

Plus, an email template that perhaps will get your email read and replied.

How do you get your music playlisted on Spotify via the UGC (user-generated content) playlists? As you might have guessed, the Spotify playlisting process is probably not what you think (no, we aren't going to randomly email Daniel Ek, the founder of Spotify, and ask if he'll listen to our new song. LOL).

First, some groundwork. I'm sure you're aware of all the heavyweight Spotify editorial playlists and how important these are for your career. It's these Spotify editorial playlists which account for the majority of playlisting followers. In other words, it's where the listeners are. So imagine if you woke up on a Friday and found yourself on a New Music Friday, PopTronix, Fresh Finds, Rap Caviar, or Pollen playlist.[65] And while you would love all the key editorial and curators at Spotify to take special note of your project and put you in all their playlists, it still might be a little early, depending where you are in your career. Or maybe not!

UGC Playlisters

There's a whole universe of Spotify UGC playlists out there, and these curators are individual people who can move the needle for you. These playlists are created by music fans—just like you and me—and some of these can have quite a following. There's no reason why you can't take the initiative and start reaching out to these UGC playlisters. In fact, it's probably a really smart idea. Here's why: Getting your song included in UGC playlists might help jumpstart the activity and streams on your song. If people start reacting well to your track, sharing it, playing your song multiple times, and saving it to their own playlists and libraries, all their activity sends messages to the Spotify algorithm. If I were to guess, the ensuing positive action and metrics on your track might sound something like this:

> Hey, Spotify AI. Knock, knock! Wakey Wakey! People are really liking this song. Let's help the artist out and put this track in other people's streams, and maybe even in some of our editorial playlists.

I love this new era of uploading your music directly to Spotify, Apple, Tidal, Amazon, YouTube, etc. There are tons of independent artists who are able to sustain themselves off streaming alone, and the streaming action and official Spotify playlisting all started somewhere. So how can you copy their success?

- First, the music was great. People responded.
- The songs and artist got discovered, maybe through an Apple, Spotify, Amazon, or Tidal curator directly. Or it could be via word of mouth or have come through Submit Hub. Who knows?
- If the song wasn't on the radar of an official content editor, maybe it first started with a few UGC playlists, then more UGC playlists, with more people sharing.
- An upward spiral and vortex began shaping, then maybe the Spotify algorithm picked up on it.
- Or maybe their song started showing up on some data reports.
- Or the person who curates a key playlist heard your song on Indie Shuffle or We Are: The Guard, and he or she was like, *Damn, I'm adding that one on Friday.*

You get the idea. Overall, it's about building awareness with your incredible music, ideally having a great live show, building the buzz, doing all the items we discussed in the 12-step program, and seeing if you can proverbially catch fire with your next release.

Momentum builds momentum.

So if your music can gain momentum, then maybe when you fill out info on the pitch form about your next track in your Spotify Artist profile, it might get the attention of the right Spotify curator and *whamo,* you'll wake up on Friday with your song in an appropriate and official Spotify playlist that might have millions of followers!

It's all about the build.

The Spotify Form

Submitting your track in Spotify's artist deck is something you need to do two to three weeks before your release. It's a simple form you can fill out once you have a Spotify artist profile. The form, as far as I understand it, both

- allows Spotify executives at the company to methodically listen by the genre they work in
- makes sure your new release populates in your fans' Release Radar playlist.

The Release Radar is a different playlist for each user, so if your fans are following you on Spotify and they diligently check out their Release Radar, you'll automatically be added to that playlist, which I think is pretty cool.

Your Artist Profile on Spotify

If you don't have access already, make sure you've claimed your artist profile in Spotify.[66] Once you have your artist profile, you can submit your music for editorial playlisting. Essentially, it's a form that will ask questions about things like:

- the genre of music
- sales points
- information about your artist project
- types of instruments used
- moods your song identifies with
- etc

The UGC and Pitching Your Songs for Other Playlists

I'm going to use an actual example here of an email I've just used in pitching one of our own releases.

We have our next single coming up from a goth/darkwave indie pop project. It's an incredible track, and I've identified a handful of perfect fit UGC playlists in Spotify where I think we might get some support.

One of the playlists I uncovered via my research is called Gothic/Cold Wave/Dark Wave/New Wave/Synth. (Yes, this is the actual name of the playlist!) Doing some easy research in the About section, I was able to find the name of the curator and also her email address, which was conveniently in her About section. I always follow the protocols previously outlined throughout the book.

And by the way, before cold calling or cold DM'ing or cold emailing anyone—I find the below to be three very good guidelines.

- I'm going to respect _____'s time.
- I'm going to try to bring ______ value within the conversation.
- I'm going to keep this as short as possible.

A big part of this particular pitch was that I had done my homework re what kind of music the curator liked, and I was pretty sure she was going to like this artist. My email to her is below. You can use it as a template and adjust as you see fit.

Subject: Gothic Toxic – New DarkWave Ballad "Song Title" (previously featured on Suicide Sheep, Consequence of Sound, etc.).

> Hi ______,
>
> We've never met before, but I'm a fan of your playlist and regularly keep tabs on it to see what you're liking. Great picks!
>
> For some quick context, I run the label and music blog We Are: The Guard, and a while back I opened the first US office of Kobalt Music Publishing and helped build the company for ten years. I've also been in the music biz for a bit, and some of my other signings also range from Grimes and TR/ST, to SOPHIE, etc.
>
> Right now, I'm working with a darkwave, indie pop, female-fronted duo called _____.
>
> We just broke our first one million Spotify streams with "___" (#1 Hype Machine song) and have had some great Spotify and Apple editorial features, with further blog/curation love from Suicide Sheep, We Found New Music, and Consequence of Sound.
>
> Our new single, "Song Title" just came out and here's the link! [Link]
>
> I definitely would love to put the song and the artist on your radar.
>
> We'd also for sure be down to reciprocate any support for your playlist via our socials, or feel free to check out the band's merch page if any of the swag here looks appealing (including some of the amazing jewelry the band makes).
>
> Here are a few links to check out along with a one-sheet.
>
> Tx...Benjamin.
>
> Spotify/Apple link
> Instagram link
> Your Name/Artist Name
> www.yourwebsite.com (and/or other socials)

In fact, even that email is probably a bit long. Keep in mind that many times, if the playlister doesn't have an email address, you'll also be reaching out to people via the socials. So further condensing that template into 3–4 sentences is even better.

While some of this is general, it's made for you to fill in the blanks or add any valuable information to. I'm pretty sure this email would get opened and hopefully the links would be clicked, because there's something happening; there's some level of activity in the email. There's an engaging subject line with some social proof. And the email, in my opinion, is sweet and short and impactful. We're also hopefully helping the curator. If curators like your music, you've just helped them out as well! it's a win for everyone.

Like I mentioned, a good rule of thumb is the shorter the email, the better. You can always make your email quick and easy with 150 brief words and then a PDF for all the other information and hype attached, like the artist's one-sheet.[67] And just to clarify, the "one-sheet" is kinda a brag sheet. It's the place to list all your wins within a visual representation. It also usually has text overlaid on the artist's press photo or artwork, and the one-sheet should answer the question "Why should I care?"

The email template above can be used for just about anything—from reaching out to an agent to securing a gig to finding an attorney to pitching for synchs.

Starting from Scratch

Like you, I'm starting from scratch with a lot of new artists, so I do a lot of research into these Spotify UGC playlists to see who might be out there to support the artist. I recommend you do the same. It's all about relationships, and if you strike up great relationships, it's likely they may be down to support you on your future releases as well. Everyone wants to be there in the beginning and say they were one of the first to support XYZ artist. That in itself is a great music discovery badge for these UGC playlisters.

There are some deeper dives on UGC playlisting and support, and I'll give you one other quick tip. However, I do cover playlisting techniques much more deeply and thoroughly in my "Release Blueprint – Digital Music Marketing" course which you can learn more about at www.BenjaminGroff.com/Release.

But in the meantime—here's a great user generated playlisting tip. You can literally reverse engineer the whole UGC playlisting process by researching artists similar to your sound. Here's how you do it. Go to Spotify and click the "Overview" section of either your artist profile or an artist that, as mentioned, is similar to you. Here you'll see a section that says "Fans Also Like" —and right here is part 1 of your research. Voila! I bet there are some artists here you'll recognize and others—not so much. Next, you can click on any of these artists and dive into the "Fans Also Like" tab. From here, go to that artist's "About" section. Now, on the right-hand side of the Spotify page—if you scroll down a little you'll see a section called "Discovered On." This shows which playlists the artist has been previously (or currently) featured on! Now, many of these playlists will be via Spotify's official editorial, however, there's going to be a great handful of playlists—which are User Generated. It's time to make some new friends, and those playlists are the ones you want to research and reach out to!

Keeping Track

Keep all this data you're collecting on a spreadsheet, or better yet, find a research assistant via UpWork and build relationship upon relationship and playlist upon playlist.

Find all the playlists you really think your song belongs on, and you might get lucky with your Google research and find out who the current curator is, along with the relevant Twitter or Instagram handle. You never know.

If you thought I was going to give you the magic bullet solution here, along with all the Spotify curators' email addresses, I'm sorry to tell you that it just doesn't really work like that. It takes time and work to build up your own list of curators and editorial people and connect with them. For sure, those relationships have helped us, because we've worked hard to get the awareness of our music to the UGC playlisters and coordinate closely with our digital distributors.

No doubt, if your digital distributor can pitch your latest release for specific playlists on Spotify, Apple, Tidal, etc., that's fantastic, but it doesn't mean it will happen. Give your distributor a head start and help out with some of the work and research. Also, you don't want to ask for their help two days before the song comes out! Ideally, you're talking to them four weeks before your release date.

Playlisting, in my experience, is a combination of

- diligently releasing amazing music,
- building your followers and engagement,
- working with your digital distributor,
- striking up relationships with UGC playlisters,
- having a strong rollout plan, which includes SubmitHub, and
- making sure you fill out those Spotify artist forms for every release—absolutely, 100 percent.
- Depending on your budget, hiring a publicist so the playlisters and curators read about you in all the "right" places. More on that below.

Pitch to Playlisters by Not Pitching Them

What? Yes—there's a strategy here. As I just mentioned, a lot of great editorial playlisters, let's be honest—probably don't even like being pitched! They would rather organically find out about your music. So, what can you do, here? One strategy is, of course, getting your music written up on some great blogs that these editorial people probably visit on a daily basis. It's momentum building momentum. For example, if an editorial playlister hears your song on say, Pigeons & Planes, and then also hears it on Hype Machine, and then maybe sees your song come through on a Spotify pitch form—and also, maybe your digital distributor is raving about your track—all those impressions add up! The takeaway is—you can chase after the "bus"—or you can already be there at the bus station when your ride shows up, if that makes sense. In other words, the more you can do your job, the better.

Shortcuts

There are no shortcuts here. Anyone who touts playlisting pay-for-play services, or who promises they can get you a guaranteed one million streams for $1,000 is, in my opinion, just a scam artist who will probably do you more harm than good. The algorithms for each DSP knows the quality of engagement a song is getting, so even if you pay some scam farm in China $1,000 to have a bank of a thousand iPhones and Android devices play your song a thousand times a day for five days to get five million streams, you're just asking for trouble. It might sound like a great idea. Sure, you'll get some shady, short-term results, but you even risk being *banned* from the DSP services for violating their terms of service agreements. It's happened!

The only shortcut here, like most things in life, is to jump in, pull up your bootstraps, buckle in, do the work, and take the long way home. You'll be glad you did.

Summary

If you build it, they (the fans, and consequently the labels and music publishers) will come. Part of that is earning your early fans and supporters and developing relationships with the right editorial playlisters and curators.

Note: This chapter was primarily about Spotify, as their UGC playlisting is a bit more robust in my experience than other digital service providers. This chapter is of course, not meant at all to diminish the great importance and essentialness of all the other digital service providers.

10

SOCIAL MEDIA MARKETING DO'S AND DON'TS

Aka be a "value giver" vs "value taker," especially for your fans.

While I may have previously touched on some of these subjects, some concepts are just so important that they bear repeating, even though there are so many other experts and gurus out there that cover this subject way better than I ever could.

To be honest, social media is not my passion. At all. I'd much rather take a walk in the forest or put on some Radiohead vinyl than set up social media campaigns. I'd even rather put my hand in a vice grip and see how much torture I can withstand....

Solid Concepts and Guidelines

Things change ever so quickly on social platforms in terms of new features and new ways of doing things, so I'll focus on concepts and guidelines which probably won't change over the next ten years like how best to spread your music and gain your first true thousand fans. Not everything here is going to be bible. What works for me as a good practice might work great for you, or you might decide to break all these rules and still have it work for you. When it comes to what works for me and the artists I work with, you can never go wrong with rule number one, which is simply this:

Provide. Tremendous. Value.

That's it! That's your mantra for social media. Case closed. End of story. And by tremendous value, I mean something that's entertaining, cool, original, thoughtful, and provides information.

The Do Section

DO provide constant and fresh material: new songs, photos, new mixes (remixes, acoustic mixes), live footage, behind-the-scenes footage, new lyrics you're working on, new information for your fans. Remember, your socials are your entertainment channel. You just don't want to say "Buy my shiz" every social media post. Treat your social media like your own branded TV channel. People are following and tuning into *you,* so give them great stuff to interface with.

DO provide value, insight, unique commentary, and something worth retweeting, liking, or sharing within your social media campaigns.

DO interact genuinely with your fans and your peers. Start a dialogue or ask a question or get your fans' opinion on something. Be part of the dialogue, not just a post-and-ghost artist. Some ideas: What should our track list be for the new album? What should our setlist be when we play in your town? Maybe run a contest or provide a downloadable multi-track of your music so fans can remix them, or provide instrumentals so your fans can make their own karaoke recordings and put them up on YouTube. You never know when a UGC fan-made video might go viral.

Engage with your fans via comments, retweets, and likes; and comment on pertinent, relevant, and valuable insights contributed by your fanbase.

DO monitor your metrics—see what's working and what's not. Cut out things that aren't working and put more time into the ones that are. This is a rule in any business, and so keep on top of what's working and what's not in your own music business career. It's now easier than ever to see exactly what your audience responds to and what no one cares about.

About 20 percent of your effort accounts for 80 percent of your business or activity, so focus on the 20 percent that is working and ditch the rest. You can also take this a step further and find out the best day of the week and time of day to post. Maybe you'll find that 7 p.m. EST is by far when most people interface with your social media, so post your juiciest stuff then.

DO create your first hundred, then five hundred, then thousand rabid, core, true fans. Engage them. They are the proverbial sneezers and evangelists of your work, and they will help take you to your next tens of thousands of fans.

DO expect that this is going to take time, work, and hard effort. It will not happen overnight, or even over a couple of months. If you're in this for real, it's going to take years. Do you believe in your music so much that you're willing to commit for a decade? That might be what it takes. Trust me. It's all exponential, so work consistently and diligently, even when it seems like nothing's happening, and you'll get to the place where a 10 percent increase means another hundred thousand followers.

DO find the right Twitter, Facebook, Snap, TikTok, or Instagram posting frequency that works for you. Seven tweets a day might be too much or it might be perfect. Once a week is certainly not enough, but one relevant post every day or so might be just right for you. It depends on what you see working the best. You'll probably find one or two social media outlets that seem to resonate best for you. As mentioned before, most of my artists live on Instagram (where most people do these days), but for some younger artists it might be TikTok, and for others it might be channels like YouTube. It's totally okay to prefer one, and it's probably beneficial for you to focus and specialize in one platform, as well as to stay active across all platforms.

DO (when you're not using smart URLs) use full links whenever you can in your social media posts. People are more likely to click on a full URL rather than a URL shortened link, because they can see where they're going. For instance, which would you rather click on www.instagram.com/YourArtistName or www.bit.ly/15QAREE? Another idea is to create your own branded URL link.

You can also use redirect links if you have a website you're directing people to. This might help people remember links. For example, I use links like

www.BenjaminGroff.com/Coach

which redirects to my Upwork profile:

www.upwork.com/o/profiles/users/_~01e36b6daa7af00a5a.

Which of those links are you going to remember or click on first?

DO consider hiring people via some of the outsourced companies mentioned in chapter 8 to help with the above. While it's important and vital for you to have a digital voice that stands out on your socials, maybe some of these people can help you create and manage the content. I always recommend outsourcing as much of your non-music creating activities as possible so you can focus on what's important—the music.

DO stand out in the crowd and be different, or in Seth Godin's words, be purple. His book *Purple Cow: Transform Your Business by Being Remarkable* is an *essential* book.

DO provide value and provide unique, quality products for your biggest fans. Your most rabid fans likely have no problem spending $75 for a deluxe fan package of, say:

- your signed vinyl
- a WAV download of the album
- a T-shirt
- VIP tickets that come along with a meet and greet

There are many great artist-and-content systems existing solely to help organize and sell these packages for you.

DO spend time making great bite-sized pieces of awesome content. Sure, it's your music that comes first, but what if you spent a dedicated amount of time each week making awesome content exclusively for your socials? MXMS, an artist I work with, did this for their rollout of "Gravedigger." They posted a special Instagram teaser rollout of nine separate pieces of amazing fifteen- to thirty-second video posts. One post went up each day—each one very artistic and mysterious or partially glitched, using their song "Gravedigger" for the music. Every day was a tease, and all nine were part of a 3 x 3 massive grid on Instagram of a single artwork. It was absolutely brilliant and culminated on the release day of the single.[68]

Remember: Be brilliant in everything you do, not just your music.

DO generally be totally awesome.

And now we have the cold and prickly DON'TS category:

The Don't Section

DON'T have someone make your social posts for you at this point (besides helping you schedule and manage posts). Make sure your social media voice is authentic and is your true voice. People can sniff that out. And if you're truly unique and special, that will come through in your digital voice. You can have someone help you get everything set up, and here's an idea—maybe you can do all your social posts for the week in one or two hours and schedule them out, freeing you up for the week to focus on your music. Just remember—at the end of the day, this really has to be *your* digital voice.

DON'T spam. Learn about permission marketing[69] from Seth Godin.

DON'T use bot programs or take the easy way out in building fans. Those never work. I know it might seem like the fast track to buy ten thousand Instagram followers, but what happens is

a) The platform you're using can detect this and may ban your profile.

b) You'll end up with ten thousand followers from a third world country. When you post, you'll have zero interaction. Your top city in socials will also show up as Karachi, Pakistan, or something like that, but it's pretty clear what's going on when your hometown is Tallahassee, FL.

Promoters, labels, publishers and fans are super hip to this, so really, don't bother. You'll just look lame and totally defeat the purpose.

Summary

Stand out, entertain, and delight in your approach to socials, just as you do with your own music. Provide as much value as you can online. You're nourishing your brand with every post, so be awesome.

Provide value.

Don't spam.

Be you—times three thousand.

11

YOUR ARTIST NAME AND SOCIAL MEDIA HANDLES

Make it easy for fans to find you.

I almost guarantee you won't find a chapter on search-engine optimization (SEO) anywhere in Don Passman's *All You Need to Know About the Music Business* book,[70] or any other, for that matter. But then again, who knows? What I do know is this chapter might be well worth reviewing, especially if you're a new artist and you're at the point where it's time to come up with a cool and identifiable artist name for your project.

> This will be your identity and your brand that you'll be investing in for the next five to twenty years, so make sure it counts.

It may or may not be surprising to find that almost every cool artist name has already been taken, even if it's your own legal name. I kid you not. You could come up with an artist name that's some incredible random bunch of words together like The Bricklayers Union of 1954, that actually does sound like a pretty cool artist name. or you could put a bit more thought into it.

Almost All the Good Names Are Gone?!

I remember working with DENM, whose real name is Mac Montgomery. DENM is on my publishing and label roster, and he was tentatively calling his project Dreamhouse. It turned out we couldn't use Dreamhouse because there was an artist from the '80s who had already released under that name, so we had to find something new; which was too bad, because that was a perfect name for his project. Mac got to work. Literally, if we were to print all our texts on the subject, we'd have dozens of pages of brainstorming ideas from Mac. And every time he thought he'd found the perfect artist name, we'd find that some other band from 1965 or 1979 that had released a few records already. Or we'd research some other cool name and find that just two months earlier, someone had started using it. Damn!

I saved all those texts, because it was frustratingly hilarious to be a "fly on the wall" watching Mac find the perfect artist name. Finally—there it was—DENM. Let me tell you—it can be a real challenge for anyone to find the perfect artist name and then also to capture all the social URLs. Because hopefully those aren't taken as well.

Easy to Find, Easy to Remember

Picking a name might sound super simple, but you'd be surprised how many artists can pick the wrong name for their project.

- Don't pick an artist name that's super hard to remember. It makes it instantly difficult for new fans to find you and/or remember it for long enough to convey to their friends. Picture the conversation. "Umm, I think they were called Scwelfelweiber or something like that."

- You're going to stick with your artist name for years, so make sure it counts—and that it will age well. In fact, before you make everything official, I recommend living with your artist name for a few weeks. Get some opinions before actually releasing under that name. You'll know in your gut when you find the right fit—it will just feel amazing.

- You want an artist name that will easily rank as the number-one search result in Google. This should be a no-brainer.

It's so obvious, right? But just the other day, I was looking for an artist I heard about called 6D. Well, you can imagine what happened when I put 6D into Google Search—nothing even close to a band. Hmmm, let's try:

- 6D + Music
- 6D + band
- 6D + London + Music + Band (because I remembered they were British)

Finally, on page 4 of Google's results, I found the link. Don't make it impossible for fans to find you! I couldn't even find 6D's website, SoundCloud page, or socials on my first five attempts! What good is your band name if people can't find you on Google?! I was ready to give up. Not the best-case scenario here, right?

Social Media Congruency

You ideally want all your social handles to be congruent, e.g., www.socialnetwork/yourartistname. If your artist name is already taken on the socials, there are other easy alternatives. In DENM's case, he uses socialmediaplatform/iamdenm across all his socials, and that works for him. Even I had problems grabbing Benjamin Groff, but I added a hyphen for one or two, which worked.

While searching, make sure you can also lock up that specific name on all your socials. And *lock in your domain name and make sure you own it!* Owning that online real estate really is vital, especially for securing user names that are the same across all your social media. So make sure you pick up your artistname.com website, and probably your .net and .org URL too. Since you're building a brand for yourself, you'll probably want these all locked up for the future, even if you're not using them today. At the very least, you'll prevent others from putting up a silly or unauthorized site such as www.yourartistname.org. Domain names are cheap at $12.99 or less for a year, so snatch them up and protect your IP (intellectual property).

You might think or assume that your artist or even legal name is available to buy as a .com right now. Chances are, believe it or not, someone may have already taken it. The domain may actually be in use, or someone might have simply thought of a cool name, snatched it up, and sat on it. I bought BenjaminGroff.com about fifteen years ago with no idea that I would ever use it, and I only launched my own blog in 2018.[71]

SEO (Search Engine Optimization)

If 6D had continued to become more and more popular, Google would likely figure this out and put them on page 1 of results. I can just hear the Google algorithm saying to itself: "Oh, people are searching for the keyword 6D and clicking on these links (the music and the artist), so let's definitely put those links higher up on the search results and ultimately on page 1. This is basically what SEO is all about.

That's right. SEO is where you enter your artist name into Google and Google, as a search engine, ideally returns your artist name on page 1 as the first search result. No doubt this will be easily accomplished if your artist name is something super unique like The Bricklayers Union of 1954. On the other hand, a famous artist like The 1975 probably took some time to get to the first page of search results.

If you are creating a band or artist name, a very smart thing to do is simply to enter that name into Google and see what search results come up. You can see what kind of competition is out there for your band name to be the number-one search result on Google. For example, if you're from Portland and your genre is house music, it's probably a really, really bad idea from a Google Search perspective to name your band Portland House. You'll be on page 15 of Google Search results after fourteen pages of real estate in Portland. Case in point, the (real) band Real Estate has a super hard time getting *anywhere near* page 1 on Google. Sure, people who are *really* looking for this artist might just search for "real estate music" on Apple Play, but why make things hard for your audience and new fans to find you?

Summary

While this chapter focuses on having an SEO-friendly artist name and locking in your social media URLs and website, the real takeaway is to also have an artist name that is unique—unique to you, unique and intriguing to new fans, and unique as a brand name, even if it's your own name. At the end of the day, you want an artist name you can feel confident in investing in for the next few decades, assuming you're a lifer and in it for the long run.

I know I am.

12

TIME TO PITCH YOUR MUSIC AND BEST PRACTICES

Plus the five most common noob mistakes, aka don't be one of those people.

If you haven't guessed it by now, there will always be plenty of people you'll be pitching along your journey. Hell, I make about ten pitches a day at minimum. It doesn't end. While we're all in the music business, we're also really in the sales business. That's right. We're always in the process of selling ourselves, our songs, and our artistry to the buyer—like a fan, a label, or a music supervisor. In fact, you can view most transactions as sales transactions. Even with a live show, you either sold the crowd that you're an amazing artist and they should buy your merch or you didn't. Or, perhaps I landed on your Apple artist profile and heard your first song. Am I sold on wanting to hear more or not?

Who Do You Pitch?

Now might be the right time to talk about how to sell yourself, particularly when it comes via email and cold pitches. Yes, you are going to be selectively pitching your music, but probably not to record labels, because you want to get the labels to call you, but that doesn't mean you won't be pitching your music.

Some of those people you pitch might be:

- music supervisors
- synch agencies

- PR people and publicity firms
- bloggers
- music publishers (potentially)
- A&R executives (if you're pitching your songs for artists to record)
- those you're looking to recruit for your own team, i.e., managers, lawyers, social media managers

I've done this for so long, and to date I probably have more than twenty thousand pitches under my belt, along with their highs and lows. I personally get pitched all the time from other people too, so a lot of what I'm about to tell you is from my perspective from both sides of the desk.

We're Always Selling

In any interaction you're involved with, you're always selling.[72] And either you're going to have a win/sale for yourself or your words and actions will persuade the person *not* to bother buying anything from you. Make sense? This doesn't mean just having an elevator pitch ready for the record company executive, but more that in everything—from relationships and dating, to negotiations with the car dealer, to influencing customer service to give you that discount, to just any interaction with someone walking down the street—you can either sell yourself with the right energy or fail the sale. Some of this is obvious, but you might likely find some real eye-openers here.

I could be pitching for a synch use, or pitching a song I publish for a big artist to cut, or pitching for a key collaboration, and the concept of sales is *important* when I want to work with a new client because I'm presenting myself and my company in the best possible light. It's the same when you want fans or merch sales or likes—you might be an artist, but you're still in sales; because you're always selling yourself, one way or another.

This does not mean selling out or jumping the shark like Fonzie did in that desperate move for ratings on *Happy Days*. Yes, that's actually where "jumping the shark" comes from.

The One-Sheet

Simply put, a one-sheet is the industry term for a one-page PDF of all the bragging rights you've acquired along the way in your career. It is used when pitching your music to just about anyone. Most importantly, the one-sheet should answer the question: Why should we care? In the one-sheet, you'll have your social numbers, accomplishments, awards, release and tour dates, along with notable media quotes. A great one-sheet is essential for social proof. It shows that people are paying attention and demonstrates why an editor, agent, publisher, or label should pay attention to you.

Assuming you'll have a successful publicity campaign via a PR or by submitting to blogs via a SubmitHub campaign, you'll have a long list of endorsements and specific quotes that you can pull and use to create it. You'll then use these one-sheets to share with the DSPs and your digital distributor to:

a) drive more playlisting,
b) help with other facets of your career, e.g., booking gigs,
c) set up for your next release.

In other words, having some great media quotes from a big media blog like: Pitchfork, The Line of Best Fit, Hilly Dilly, Paper, We Are: The Guard,[73] Billboard, or even smaller bloggers, can help prime your next release and draw attention to it.

A one-sheet helps these outlets pre-vet you. Whoever is on the receiving end of your one-sheet might have some internal dialogue like, *Oh wow, that music blog, We Found New Music, posted about them and raved about them. Okay. I'll pay attention.*

To put this within the context of another social proof example: you just don't want to be the single guy walking in and sitting at a bar without any friends. A w k w a r d. Conversely, that same guy or gal walking into the bar with a bunch of friends and giving high fives with confidence, who is showing that everyone already likes him or her aka social proof, could get everyone asking "Who is that person? I wanna join their party!" If you have a great one-sheet with some great blog posts, "Yeah! I'm somebody now!"[74]

Pitching That Works

I've experimented a lot, and at least for me, I've found what works and what to avoid. The following are key things to keep in mind when pitching your music. It doesn't matter who you're pitching to, either online or in person.

You just don't want to end up in the proverbial trash.

I'm giving you these pointers straight up. Today's new music business is radically different than it was even five years ago, but overall, one big theme to keep in mind is just to respect the other person receiving your pitch.

Respecting people for who they are, and also their time, will get you a long way.

1. PLEASE DON'T SEND OR PITCH MORE THAN THREE OR (REALLY) FOUR SONGS AT ONCE.

In fact, maybe start with just one or two songs. If you think you have one amazing, no-brainer smash, just send that one. That's actually a *great* way to get someone's focus. Time and time again, I've been able to kick in a closed door with just *one* hit, attention-getting song.

This is more of a songwriting / pitching story, but it's actually how I got my first cut as a music publisher, and consequently my first Billboard Top 10 hit! It was 1996/1997, and I received an amazing song called "Invisible Man" written by Steve Kipner, Sean Hosein, and Dane Deviller. I sent just this one song to every record label president. I thought the song was *so* good, and it *was*. Lo and behold, Andre Harrell, president of Motown at the time, actually listened and called me back. At the time I was just a twenty-four-year-old noob in the music business, so it was a big deal for me. Consequently, the song ended up being the debut single for 98 Degrees, and my first hit as a music publisher. I learned the power of kicking in the door with just one song, which is especially possible when you have an amazing one.

It's so easy to listen to just one song. It's quite another when you send a link of ten songs with no mention of which song to focus on. Executives don't have time for ten songs! We just care about the one career song that will awaken a fan base and has the *wow* effect. If you have difficulty objectively figuring out which song is the best, you can get feedback and opinions from your friends, colleagues, or the cold and cruel heart of the internet—which is even better. But if you can't keep yourself from sending just one song ... start with only your three best.

The subtext of sending an email is the following: You're asking for their time and attention. Often unsolicited. For example, imagine you're walking down the street and someone just randomly interrupts you, requesting you hear their important song gospel. I'm sure that in most cases, you couldn't be bothered with whatever they're handing out, even if it's five-dollar bills. I'm not kidding. I bet 75 percent of people would just walk by, even if you're handing out free money. It's very similar to interrupting an executive just trying to get through a list of priorities for the day. So structure your email in a way that takes minimal time to read and also makes them feel like you are bringing value to them with your great songs. This way you'll have a much better opportunity of your song being heard. There's a way to do this, and I'll get there in the next few pages.

2. SEND LINKS THAT ARE RECOGNIZABLE AND CAN STREAM INSTANTLY, MP3S...MAYBE.

You want to make it easy for your music to actually get heard. MP3 attachments can clog up email systems. WeTransfer links mean someone has to click on something, then download the files, then find them on their computer or on their phone. At least for me on my phone, I never know where those downloads go—so I can't even play them. And trust me, people are wary of downloading any files from strangers. Some companies won't even allow their employees to click download links.

Why not make it easy and create a SongSpace,[75] SoundCloud,[76] Box,[77] or Dropbox[78] account? Make a three-song set of your music with a link you can easily send and which can be streamed instantly (or if they choose, that they can also download). For Brill Building, my publishing company, we use SongSpace. In my opinion, it's the best tool to keep a private library and track if someone has heard or downloaded your song. It's also a great platform to keep a record of other key metadata, lyrics, and co-write information tied to your copyright. While this is mostly a streaming-based service, there's also an option to download the file.

3. DON'T PITCH ON A WEEKEND.

I automatically know that anyone who pitches on the weekend is usually a part-time hobbyist artist and a weekend warrior of making music. This might sound harsh, but if you pitch me something on the weekend, I almost automatically know it's going to be bad. Ninety-five percent of the emails I receive that come in on the weekend often end up being deleted or sent to junk mail. Sorry. I'm just telling you the truth. Sure, the weekends might be the only time you have to do your pitching, but don't make us think that! Plus, by sending emails on the weekend, the subtext of that email to the executive is also, "Hey, I know you're trying to relax and not look at your inbox on the weekend, but look, I'm going to make you work anyway." Again, the overall thought on pitching is to respect the other person receiving your pitch.

Send emails during the week during business hours. I would also recommend not sending pitch emails on a Monday, when so much of the week's mania is starting for most executives. I would also avoid Friday after 1 p.m. It's around this time that people are cleaning up for the weekend and don't need to receive more work from you.

Hint: If you have a day job that doesn't allow you to send emails or pitches during the day, just set up the parameters in your Outlook, or other email services like Boomerang for Gmail, to schedule your emails to be sent on a specific date and time. I do it all the time myself, especially with international pitches.

My Little Friend, Boomerang

Boomerang for Gmail is my number-one productivity tool. For example, if I'm sending a pitch, and the person I'm sending it to is based in London or Seoul, I'll set up the email so it will specifically arrive in their inbox at 11:30 a.m. or 3:30 p.m.—before or after their lunch—during their workday. Otherwise I'd have to stay up into the wee morning hours of the night, like 4:30 a.m., to send emails to the UK—if I want them to arrive at the right target time.

The percentage of emails read and, more importantly, songs being heard, is much higher when you provide an easily listenable streaming link and when your emails arrive during normal business hours.

To boot, Boomerang for Gmail has an awesome bonus in their system—also called Boomerang. Essentially, for each email you send, you can opt for it to be boomeranged back if your recipient hasn't responded. You can choose for the email to be boomeranged back to you in one day, one week, three weeks and two days ... whatever! Let's put this in perspective, too. In some cases, my team and I have spent a full hour or more on a pitch full of juicy ideas and hit songs. And then we send out the pitch ... and time goes by. *Tick tock. Tick tock.* But then we're usually on to the next urgent thing. A week goes by and we may have forgotten about that pitch we made that we spent so much time to get just right. To boot, that pitch may result in a million-dollar opportunity. So should we just let it go into the ether? *Hell no!*

There have been numerous times I've been able to turn a nonresponse into an actual yes simply by having that pitch boomeranged back to me. This reminds me to resend the email with a polite "Hey ___, just wanted to make sure you got the below" follow-up. It takes another thirty seconds on top of the hour I invested in the pitch, and we've potentially made the artist hundreds of thousands of dollars, if not more.

I talked about not pitching on the weekend, so personally, on a weekend, I might set up thirty to fifty emails that get delivered throughout the week at specific times. Many of these aren't even pitches. They could be follow-ups or responses. This also applies to my employees and consultants, because for sure, I respect them as well. I don't want their weekend fun to be zapped by an email that can 100 percent wait until Monday.

4. DON'T ASK FOR PERMISSION.

This is one of my pet peeves. So many "how to pitch your demo" type of lame-o, old-school books say you should call or email for permission to send some music. In other words, get permission first so it's not unsolicited material. I'm telling you that this is totally wrong. Pending your level of political correctness, this is like going out on a date and at the most romantic moment, will all willing participants, asking, "Hey, is it okay to hold your hand? Please fill out this consent form." Not confident.

How many rock stars do you know who ask for permission? Exactly. If you're asking permission to send your stuff, I already know that the music is not good enough, because you're not confident enough yourself to send it. Flip the script. Yeah, it's that executive who's going to be the lucky one hearing your music!

5. NO LAME NAME-DROPPING PLEASE.

This is more for the songwriters looking to get a publishing deal. *Don't* name-drop who you are writing with or who you know. If this is the only hype and promotion in your arsenal, we'll automatically know you don't have anything better to talk about, like your released songs or your songs recorded by other artists. We look for the emails or discussions about your forthcoming confirmed cuts, releases, or songs that have just hit the radio. Yeah, it helps to know who you're writing with if they're meaningful, but you'd be surprised how many emails I get from aspiring songwriters who are hyping names of people they're working with who also don't have anything going on.

If you're an artist, you want to promote the fact that you're getting your first million streams or that you have your first hundred thousand monthly listeners on Spotify, not the names of people you think are important. That's a great start and will get our attention.

Summary

There's a right way and a wrong way to pitch yourself and your music. There's also a mindset and confidence that comes along with this.[79] As a golden rule, remember to respect other people and put your best foot forward. And with that best foot, that's how you kick in the door.

13

THE PR/PUBLICITY LOVE AND HATE RELATIONSHIP

If I could snap my fingers and get all my money back...

Who They Are & Why You Should or Shouldn't Hire Them?

Today's the day. You have finally put the finishing touch on that amazing single, EP, or album— you know, that piece of work that took all your blood, sweat, tears, and money to make. You've arrived. Your music is here! So you're probably asking how you now get the world to know about your music.

If you want exposure, a great publicist can be one of your best friends. Conversely, I'll say from my own experience that a publicist can also be one of the biggest money-sucking investments you can make. *Wait. What?*

No doubt, a great publicist on your team can be a huge score, but who are these people? Publicists, often called PR or public relations people, are those who have key relationships with music bloggers, media outlets, lifestyle brands and companies, late-night television show producers (for shows like Conan, Kimmel, Corden) and even some DSPs (like Apple, Spotify, Amazon curators). *However,* if I could snap my fingers and make a wish, it would be to get back all the money given to lame PR people and firms. If you really want to lose $5,000 very fast, just hire a mediocre publicist early in your career, especially when there's no story to tell. Literally, I've spent at least $25,000 over the years that just went up in smoke, with only a few dozen blog posts to show for it. How would you like to know you spent almost $1,000 on each blog post...?

I simply won't take that statement back. New artists actually getting a return on their PR investment at an early stage in their artist career is unlikely. As for my own label releases, I've put the kibosh on hiring publicists for new artists. It's not even a consideration anymore.

In the same breath, it's worth noting I've had some fantastic, amazing, and *epic* results with publicists who truly over delivered. But really, that's a rare occasion. It's an ongoing joke with at least one of my clients. "Hey, you wanna hire a publicist who'll just take our money and send out an email blast which no one will ever read?" I know this because I'm actually on all those PR blast lists, and after diligently going through them for months, I had to give up on ever reading them again. It was just too much high quantity vs. low quality of music releases.

To iterate my position, those of you who are publicists and know how great of a PR job you do, *thumbs up!* I *love* you. I so value your hard work and what you bring to the table. You're worth your weight in gold. In many cases you have been pivotal in breaking open an artist's career, and you remain vital to many artists' successes to this day. On the other hand, those of you who just took my, and my artists', money and ran ... you know who you are. My ratio so far has been one great experience for every seven.

Again, as a general rule, I'm not hiring publicists for new artists. We're usually starting from square one—like zero or close to zero, and there's barely a story yet to talk about. Yet. We'd get no return on investment, and there are so many other more profitable things we could be spending money on at this point in an artist's career.

The Costs

A solid, well-respected PR person, might run you $750–$1,000 to work one song. As far as a return on those costs, you would need about 250,000 Spotify streams to just break even. Hey, that just might happen! But don't forget all your other costs in the equation too, costs you need to recoup with those streams as well.

The better PR firms want $2,500+ for a three-month commitment ($7,500), which would mean you'd need 1,500,000 Apple streams to break even on that investment … just for PR. Again, that could totally happen, but I generally prefer to spend money on PR only when there's already some type of artist following, a story to tell, more robust socials, and a catalog of songs—a mix of things that benefit from the new PR attention. For instance, if you promote your very first single ever vs. your catalog of four albums, you'll benefit more with the latter as more people discover your other material. In other words, if you have a fully stocked grocery store, it makes more sense to commit a robust advertising budget vs. an unproven produce stand on the corner with only one tomato to sell.

I'm also more comfortable hiring a publicist if there's some sort of identifiable culture around the artist. The combination of great music, culture, strong socials, and also a visual identity can really set the wind to your back here if you get a PR firm or individual publicist on board. Blogs and media love highly visual artists for photo shoots, deep interviews, etc. Simply put, it makes the publicist's job way easier to promote you. There's a story! And you'll probably have more success in getting features and write-ups because you're that much more interesting to write about. Period.

Which is why it's so, so, *so* important to *stand out.*

Don't get me wrong; you could have the most amazing new EP or single, a new story to tell, and be amazingly culturally relevant, and your first single is the most written-up song of that week. It absolutely happens, and I've been involved with some of those. However, it's been my experience that these media outlets and blogs will usually focus first on artists who have something actually going on.

Let's put it into perspective. These music blogs and media outlets only make money through page views and advertising, so why should they give up real estate on their website for new artists who might only bring in ten page views from their fanbase? On the other hand, that same blog might do a premiere with a more established artist, or an artist who has a massive buzz happening, and that artist might be able to bring ten-thousand page views to the music blog. Crunching the numbers, if that media outlet is getting $7.50 per thousand page views (CPM) on their ads, that's $75 to $150 of income that music blog or media outlet can potentially make on a three hundred- to thousand-word post over a few days. These blogs are working within their business model. They want page views and web traffic to drive revenue via advertising. It's never just about the music for bigger blogs and media outlets.

Wait ... isn't that a catch-22? Even if I hire a publicist, I might not get my music exposed? Isn't that their job?!

A Possible Solution

1. First, make sure you're bringing all those things I previously talked about in the twelve steps.

2. Then, for your own releases, instead of hiring a publicist, use SubmitHub.com. We use Submit Hub for every release, and as previously mentioned, I've been able to get one of our recent singles a number-one slot on the Hype Machine just by spending $150 on SubmitHub.com. Now that is an *amazing* return on investment! Phenomenal! *Kapow!*

3. Additionally, instead of hiring a PR firm, I'd rather take that same $750 to $3,000 and invest it in social media advertising, aka digital marketing: Instagram Story ads, Facebook ads, YouTube video ads.

But let's say you're beyond just a simple starting point and you have a decent following. Yes, you've followed the steps in this book to acquire your first thousand true fans. Great! You might be ready to hire that PR person for some bigger looks. To promote an EP or an album, it can cost:

- $750 to $1,000 to promote one song, to
- upwards of $2,000 to $3,500 a month for a suggested three-month campaign.

At this point, it might be well worth getting that PR firm involved.

One of the other benefits of a great PR will be all the juicy media quotes you'll be able to pull, providing credibility to push forward your career. And you'll be able to use all these quotes for your one-sheet I talked about in chapter 12.

As mentioned, one ancillary great thing about PR firms is that at the end of a campaign, they'll give you a list of all the blogs and media outlets who wrote you up, and you can pull quotes from there to add to your next one-sheet. Of course, you can also get these quotes with that $100 to $150 SubmitHub campaign, assuming the blogs and media outlets decided to write you up. And, of course, you can also find all of that through your friend the Google.

Google Alerts

At this point in time, it's probably smart to go to Google Alerts[80] and set up daily or weekly reporting on your artist project. Basically, any time your artist name is mentioned, you'll be alerted. It's a great way to keep track of those outlets who praised you, and it's also important to give reciprocal shoutouts back with thanks on your socials plus a link to the article. Always remember to give thanks. Those pieces of gratitude mean a lot and add up in the eyes of the gratitude universe. No doubt, if you can drive some traffic back to these people who showed you some love, they'll love you even more.

Summary

The right PR firm and/or individual publicists who *believe* in you, *and* who want to wholeheartedly roll up their sleeves to jumpstart your career, can be phenomenal. On the other hand, if you're just in the early stages of your career, it's probably more important to find your culture and artist identity; and to focus on building your undeniable material, winning videos, amazing songs, social following, and SubmitHub submissions.

You'll know when the time is right to take that next step and hire a great publicist. In fact, if you've done your job right, it's entirely possible that they'll be reaching out to you, which is the premise of this book. If you create the right sparks, the fire will come.

My takeaway here is a PR testing barometer. You'll know the time is right to hire someone if that person is a genuine fan and who will go to the nth degree to promote your music. That's also what it will take. Passion. Belief. Genuine excitement. This is counter to the PR person who just needs your check to help pay the telephone bill for the month, which happens all the time. It's a major difference which provides majorly different results. When it comes to building any members of your team, gravitate to those most passionate about your art and career. You simply just can't buy that stuff.

The Go-To PR Firms. Who Are They?

While these firms can be ever changing, I've done some of the research for you. Some PR firms are more geared toward indie, electronic, alternative, and indie pop music than others. It's up to you to focus on which firms are right for you and to do the due diligence, but I'll give you a pretty big head start. Now, if you're looking for a metal, jazz, or country publicity person; or if you're not in the US, you'll have to do some more online research. It's just not my key bread and butter.

Note: You'll probably only have success in hiring one of these firms if you already have solid momentum behind you. PR firms have their own reputations on the line, and they need that story to tell, so most PR firms will not just pick up anyone. On the other hand, publicists also need new clients to help pay the bills and keep the lights on, which is why I am cautious in hiring PR firms at an early stage of anyone's career.

Go-To PR Firms

Here are some of my favorites, in no particular order. (Note that for sure, their artist rosters will have changed somewhat by the time you're reading this—but you'll get the idea).

Girlie Action

Music marketing and management. One of the other well-known and long-standing digital marketers based in New York City.

Website: www.girlieaction.com
Roster: Tori Amos, Santigold, Trentmøller, Shamir, Kid Koala, Dita Von Teese, Elliott Smith.

Magnum PR

Magnum PR has more of a focus on publicity, but they also provide digital marketing services.

Website: magnumpr.net
Clients: The Glitch Mob, Shift K3y, Tribe Society, Loudpvck.

Biz 3

One of the top taste-making companies in the industry. They have a diverse roster of over 100 artists, authors, filmmakers, and visual artists. They are well connected with magazine editors, key people at large national publications, and TV channels. They also promote artists through film and DVD projects, books, websites, new media ventures, festivals, and parties.

Website: biz3.net
Clients: $uicideBoy$, Anderson. Paak, Babymetal, Black Eyed Peas, Col3trane, G-Eazy, Danny Brown, Justice, OWSLA, A-Trak, Amanda Blank, Psalm One, Asher Roth, Skrillex, Teddybears, Crystal Castles, Maluca, The Raveonettes, White Denim, and Uffie.

No Big Deal PR

No Big Deal PR has established a track record in the music industry as a results-focused and competitive publicity firm.

Website: nobigdealpr.com
Clients: Anna of the North, Aly & AJ, Ames, Cheat Codes, Demo Tapes.

Fancy PR

Fancy PR is a boutique full-service public relations agency that works across industries including tech, ad agencies, consumer brands, fashion, non-profits, and editorial.

Website: www.fancypr.com/clients
Clients: Sofi Tukker, Rhye, Mt. Joy, Miami Horror, Goldroom, Great Good Fine OK.

KLUTCH

KLUTCH is an L.A.-based full-service public relation, marketing, brand strategy, and creative consulting company.

Website: klutchpr.com
Clients: Cheat Codes, Goldhouse, Junior Prom, FRND, Gabriel Alpin.

Unfolded PR

A public relations agency focused on dance music.

Website: beunfolded.com
Clients: Arno Cost, Bobby Puma, Breathe Carolina, Dirty Soul, Dirty South, DVBBS, Flamingo Recordings.

Black Panda

Black Panda PR is a full-service music publicity and consulting firm.

Website: blackpandapr.com
Clients: Bibi Bourelly, Brandyn Burnette, Galactic, Ghost Loft, LAUV, Melanie Martinez, Missio.

14

MUSIC PUBLISHERS

This has been my job for 25 + years!

Who Are They, What They Do and Why You Should Care?

I know this is a book on getting a record deal and securing your first thousand true fans, but a great music publisher can be a huge ally for your artist project. You will need a music publisher at some point in your career, even if it's just to administrate and collect your royalties. If your goal is to additionally secure a music publishing contract, this chapter will be great for you. And we're going to follow the same principles here—as far as standing out, and having something "going on" that gets their attention—so *they* end up calling *you*, right?!

Music publishers are often, in my opinion, more switched on when it comes to music discovery. They're savvy and have their ears to the ground more than a lot of record label A&Rs. Additionally, there are few out there, *ahem,* who are willing to take risks and bet on someone's career a little earlier on. If you're creating the right buzz and metrics, prepare for that call.

Songwriting and Song Copyrights

As a quick definition, a music publisher signs you for your songwriting and song copyrights, as opposed to the record labels working with you and signing your masters, aka your master studio recordings.

Music publishing is all about your songs, lyrics, and music compositions. It's the publisher's job to first and foremost collect your songwriting and publishing royalties, but ideally, as well, help develop and make key connections for you. This means hooking you up with other key co-writers; making introductions to producers, record labels, managers; and pitching your music.

Pitching

A great music publisher is like a great agent for your songwriting. Music publishers pitch your songs for film/TV/ads synchronization uses, or for other artists to record (like Britney Spears and Rihanna, who don't write their own songs). In fact, most major music publishing companies all have their own internal film and TV department—a bonus, right?

Some of the artists I've placed songs with or arranged artist cowrites with are Beyoncé, Britney Spears, Kelly Clarkson, Eric Clapton, Charli XCX, Demi Lovato, Selena Gomez, BB King, Christina Aguilera, G-Eazy, and BTS. While I was at Kobalt, our synchronization team landed tremendous synch placements for OneRepublic. Ryan became a famous songwriter but also wrote for others—songs such as "Halo" for Beyoncé, "Sucker" for Jonas Brothers, and "Bleeding Love" for Leona Lewis. We also landed key collaborations for him with great artists, even Adele!

Introductions

Music publishers can help make the right introductions to

- record labels—not just domestically, but internationally as well,
- distributors,
- digital marketers,
- A&R execs,
- attorneys,
- managers,
- other co-writers,
- producers,
- mixers,
- mastering people.

A music publisher may be able to, just in a few calls, make a personal connection for you with a key record label executive—a connection that may have taken years for you to achieve on your own, if at all. Ideally, you can work with a music publisher who's known as an authority and tastemaker, whom other executives in the music industry trust.

Co-Publishing

A music publisher also can provide a monetary advance. Cha-Ching! Just as labels will give you an advance to sign and release your masters, a publisher will give you an advance in exchange for coownership of your copyrights (called a co-publishing deal). Publishers give you an advance whereby they co-own the songs with you and put their own sweat equity and personal investment into you and your work. Ideally, they will also be active in pitching your music.

Just make sure you know what you're getting into when you sign a contract, as there are many internal clauses within a co-publishing deal that may or may not be attractive long term, such as minimum delivery commitments (which can sometimes be difficult to achieve), internal surcharges on your royalties, etc. Publishers usually take a commission rate of around 25 to 35 percent on co-publishing deals, depending on if they procured activity/got you a placement on a specific song.

Administration Deals

A publisher may only administer and collect your royalties but not have ownership in your songs, which is called an administration deal. The rates for this type of deal range from 10 to 20 percent; however this all depends on the actual company, as well as the amount of advance the publisher is willing to give you up front. Administration deals are designed to be no-risk financial deals for the publisher, so sometimes advances can be zero. However, often the publisher may offer a conservative advance based on royalties they can immediately collect for you.

Regardless if it's a co-publishing deal, an administration deal, or even a record deal, if you really feel someone is going to champion your music and move your career ahead five years faster than you could on your own, it's worth striking up a deal and working with that person. Their passion for your project is always a leading indicator of a potentially fruitful relationship, but as always, consult with a lawyer.

But the mantra of this book is not to chase music publishers and record labels empty-handed. You want those executives to hear your buzz via the tools presented in this book and for them to call you. And if you are going to reach out to them, you need to have some bullet-point success points that will validate your music and encourage anyone reading your email to readily click on your links. In other words, you already want to be on the way to being a success before you ever start reaching out to these people.

If you do reach out and pitch yourself to publishers, remember to use that one-sheet.

Music Publishers—Key Players

Some of the best and biggest music publishing companies to look into are the following:

- Universal
- Sony/ATV
- Warner/Chappell
- BMG Rights

Major Indie Music Publishers

- Kobalt Music—actually bigger on the charts than many of the majors, and the company I worked at for ten years, opening the first office in the United States
- Peer Music
- Pulse Music Publishing
- Prescription
- Zync/Round Hill
- Downtown
- APG
- Ten Music Group

Boutique Music Publishers

There are a few out there, but I really feel Brill Building represents and nurtures some of the best new artists and writers on the scene (my 100-percent-owned music publishing company).[81] I have a small roster of about twenty clients, and between myself and our family-style executive staff, we really provide that roll-up-the-sleeves, sweat equity, and hard-work mentality for our clients. And we take early risks on writers, producers, and artists—something the majors certainly don't do much of anymore.

A few favorite publishers in the boutique lane (twenty clients or less) would be:

- MXM Publishing or Wolf Cousins (Max Martin's music publishing company)
- Camelot Music Group (hit writer, Evan Bogart's publishing company)
- Blotter Music (great early developer of talent, Steve Lindsey's music publishing company)
- Unrestricted (Ben Madahi's company)

Regarding the above companies, you might be wondering how to reach out to them. Some internet searches will find you the right email addresses and staff member names. There's also an excellent registry book for music publishers, record label executives, and even music supervisors and synch executives that you can buy at the Music Business Registry. [82] This is the industry contact bible—the most complete, up-to-date, and reliable directory for the music business. In many cases, it even has the names and emails address of the assistants.

Summary

Music publishers can be a great ally in building and breaking out your career as an artist, writer, or producer, and sometimes even both. And yes, you can be both an artist *and* writer for other artists as well.

As a music publisher for more than twenty-five years myself, the tasks in this chapter are entirely what my daily workflow entails. Ultimately, besides collecting your songwriting royalties and providing advances to quit your day gig, a music publisher can be a hero and ally as it relates to your songwriting endeavors, with their deep relationships in the music business linking you up with key creative partners.

15

TO TIKTOK OR NOT TO TIKTOK?

This book wouldn't be complete without a chapter on TikTok. In fact, I've contemplated making an entire digital course on the subject or who knows, even starting a TikTok influencer agency. TikTok is already huge - and I think it's actually just getting started.

Now, depending on the genre you're in - you might be thinking...*"Should I invest in TikTok as a platform?"* The short answer is YES! In my opinion, it doesn't matter the genre you're in ... the growth and popularity of the platform is exploding. You can be sure there's a corner of TikTok just for you and your music.

Now - some quick background on TikTok before we dive in.

TikTok used to be an app called Musical.ly, and the Musical.ly app was geared more towards a tween demographic (think 10-15 year olds making original lip sync style videos and challenges). The new brand of TikTok, however - is something completely different.

Basically, people create videos using the TikTok app, which features around 15 or more seconds of a song (or in TikTok's case what they call a "sound"). You can use the audio "sound" of another user's video as well - and this is important, as I'll explain later, as it's important to "seed" the audio with the right influencers.

This is Not Your Little Niece's Musical.ly

TikTok today is not just about challenges, dance videos and skits. There's a whole slew of educational videos, informational content, cooking tips, jokes, science, health influencers in every sector, and so much more. I've even taken the leap here for some branded educational / insider music business and songwriting videos. You can check those out here: @Benjamin.Groff.

Now, *especially* for music, TikTok is a lot different than say, a passive listening experience on a Spotify or Apple playlist. On TikTok, people are actually creating video content and interacting with your songs and "sounds."

#TikTok Challenge - What A Great Idea!

Before we dive further into TikTok, just - one thing. Whenever I set up a release plan or talk about artists on how we're going to "catch fire" with a new release - the topic always comes up. "Hey - I have a *great* idea. We could do a TikTok #challenge." Me: What? I had no idea? Yes! And we could also make a viral video!" (That was sarcasm there fyi). Meaning - anyone who ever set out to make a viral video - probably never *ever* made a viral video.

In my opinion - TikTok challenges don't really work like this.

If you're a fairly new artist with a small to medium following - yes, for sure, you can do your TikTok #challenge - but it's like that proverbial tree that falls in a forest - with no one to hear it, does it really make a sound? You can be a new artist and run a TikTok challenge and seek virality - but take note - for the best chance of success, your song really NEEDS TO BE SEEDED with the right TikTok influencers.

This is the new game today and *this* is what major labels are spending crazy tons of money on. A TikTok campaign can easily start at $5,000 per song and I heard a major label, for a brand new artist, just spent $30,000 for one campaign. In fact, the rumor is ... to really move the needle - you might need upwards of $20,000 - $30,000. At least, that's the sandbox the majors are playing in on costs (from what I hear).

TikTok = Seed + Harvest

Here's how it works - many of the top influencers are managed by TikTok influencer agencies. These agencies have direct access to influencers from their roster and consequently, of course, their audiences. Upon hire, these agents will pay the influencers they represent, to start your #challenge or have those influencers use your song in some creative way on the platform. Not only will the influencers make a TikTok video, but *as* importantly, the influencer will also *seed your song* - meaning your audio clip aka "the sound" will now be available on that influencer's profile for others to grab and use!

Think of this as a bonus. First, the influencers are making a video using your song. Secondly, they're posting the actual "sound" on their profile aka your audio - for others to use!

Notably - this is how your song "gets" into TikTok and how others can discover your music. Right now, if not mistaken, the songs that you can *officially* use in TikTok's library are pretty much the major label's hits and the biggest songs of the day. It's not like Spotify or Apple, where your song is just *instantly* on the TikTok app. So having your "sound" seeded by an influencer is huge. At least this is how it works for now.

Legal Payola

Also - in my opinion, think of this as "legal payola." Actually, I'm sure the labels are thinking of TikTok exactly that way. LOL. In fact, it might be better than payola! (And BTW, what is payola? Payola is a very illegal practice whereby record labels would pay cash or provide other juicy incentives to radio stations, programming directors and the like - to play their artist's songs on the radio). Now - in the old days, maybe some "under the table" bucks would get your new single added to that station's commercial radio rotation. Of course, especially in the old days before digital tracking, it might be hard to tell if the radio station actually delivered - or maybe they gave you just that 1 spin rotation at 3:30 am on a Sunday night. Big deal.

However on TikTok - it's *guaranteed* that the influencer is absolutely going to make a TikTok video of your song, do the #challenge you've requested or simply feature the song in a TikTok upload and tag you. If the influencer doesn't do this - then, you don't pay!

Return on Investment

If you do have the bucks for a campaign, and the right content to back it up - it's a no brainer, in my opinion, to spend $5,000 to $10,000 to potentially make $100,000 or more. Of course, this 20X return on investment doesn't happen all the time! That being said, I do have a song via my publishing company that's taking off right now on Spotify! The artist's label (which is an indie, by the way) has paid for the song to be seeded exactly as I've just described. The song is *exploding* (like 5 Millions streams a day)!

The other thing to keep in mind is the process is fast! Almost overnight (or certainly within the launch week), you'll have a pretty good idea, if your song is going to get any serious traction.

And those are just a few reasons why every major record label (including my own indie pop label, We Are: The Guard) has made TikTok a top priority. And so should you. I would strongly consider this, even if you're the coolest indie rock band from Credsville, Seattle (as I'll explain further).

Pro Tip!

So - investing in TikTok - YES! At a minimum, I would be developing your profile and uploading fresh content every day. A good pro tip is to keep your content to 15 seconds or less. Why? There simply will be more people watching 100% of a short 15 second clip, than say a .55 second video. In other words, the algorithm is being told 95% of people are watching 100% of this video vs 36% of people who watched 100% of the .55 second video. Which TikTok do you think the algorithm is going to favor? Make sense?!

Make TikTok Work For You

But trying to launch that that #challenge on your Instagram that has under 5,000 followers? Hmm. Maybe? Unless the #challenge is crazy original and *incredible,* I wouldn't expect overnight success - but hey, it can happen! But moreso, building a following on TikTok - no matter what the genre - is something I suggest you do.

Now, you might be thinking - "Well, I'm in a screamo death metal band - TikTok is not for me!" Maybe?! Or *maybe* you're one of the handful of death metal bands that all the death metal fans on TikTok happen to find and embrace and spread the word. Remember - TikTok is just not for hip hop and Top 40! Your audience (or potential audience) is on TikTok *somewhere!*

Personally, for myself - I'd love to be *"the"* songwriting / music publishing / label influencer on TikTok. Thus, I'm making the investment. I'm going for it. It's a wide open field right now!

As a label, I've just kicked off my 2nd TikTok campaign for a new single release. The first one we did was a song called "Lifted" by an artist called Butter, back in the Musical.ly days. We made a little choreographed dance, seeded it appropriately and thus, have had well over 6 Million Spotify streams. It worked!

Bottom line "you gotta spend - to see what you get in the end." (I just made that little ditty up).

And as far as investments and getting the most bang for your buck - if it's the right type of song, and the right type of challenge or idea ... I suggest you explore this. For the latest release I just mentioned - we have $5,000 set aside for the promotion. We're putting it ALL IN on TikTok. Why? We have the right song and an amazing #challenge. We've also, already shot the "#challenge for other influencers to use (it looks great) and, the artist already has like 500,000 followers on the platform. So yeah, we have a little head start, to say the least. All this considered, It would be crazy for us to *not* place a bet using TikTok as a focal promotion piece. It's an exponential return on investment if it lights up and we get it right!

Obviously, it's going to be up to you to assess if such a promotional spend is warranted.

Lastly, as a bonus to this chapter - below are some observations of what generally works on the platform. And while these bullet points are really more reflective of hip hop and pop stories - certainly there are success stories in your genre. Or maybe you just need to create them and be the latest success story!

TikTok Guidelines / Thoughts

- Get on the app! Get used to it. It's here to stay (assuming it won't get banned for security issues) - and the growth happening on TikTok is astounding!
- Identify the key trends and influencers.
- Avoid explicit lyrics. This is a younger crowd and TikTok has previously censored language. Play it safe and make sure to have a clean version.
- Hip Hop is the primary genre for now, though pop and indie have a place, too.
- Remember that some TikTok songs don't even use real words (we're looking at you, bbno$).
- Keep it simple lyrically - but still fire! Make it easy for people to sing along and create choreography that matches what you're saying.
- Keep it upbeat! Most of the songs are danceable, high energy, and fun (though there are a few exceptions).

TikTok Writing Elements

Try to use one or more of the following key elements:

- Raw / Extreme Sounds
- A solid beat / drop or space for a dramatic reveal or a scene swap
- A standout social-media-content-creatable-line
- Ask users to do something ("Wipe It Down," "Flip the switch")
- Skits / Spoken Word Content

Hope that was helpful!

Summary

So, to answer the question kicking off the beginning of this chapter: "To TikTok or Not to TikTok?"

The answer is simple.

TikTok.

PART 4

FIN

16

THE END GAME AND NEW STARTING POINT

When to actually sign to a label deal?

Now that you've read most of the book—and maybe you're even starting to have some success in your career, I suppose you might have one (or two or three) really gigantic questions on your mind:

> What if all this really happens?!
>
> What if all the labels get in a panic to sign me?
>
> What happens if I do all this work and create that spark, and things really start catching fire?

By fire, I mean a track getting fifty thousand-plus streams a day, or a video going viral, or your new release magically securing a $30,000 film trailer, or a number-one Hype Machine song, or a Pitchfork write-up.... In other words, *Holy crap. All this hard work I put in and it's happening! Now what?!*

Remember that part I told you about your contact info—making it easy for people to find you and checking in to read your emails every day? Well, I can tell you for sure that what's going to happen next is your inbox is going to start blowing up. That's a good thing! That's the whole goal of this process and book—getting them, whoever they may be, to call you. Now when you open your inbox, for sure these emails will range from people who are genuinely super passionate and love what you're doing to those that are just practically spamming you. On that note, these emails will generally fall into two buckets:

a) The first crowd will want to help support you, get involved, provide advances and opportunities, or maybe be a new partner. You might hear from a manager, agent, or attorney who wants to represent you, or maybe even a new creative collaborator or a promoter offering you a tour or festival gig.

b) You'll also get what I call robo emails. These are copy-paste type emails probably written up by interns or creative assistants. These emails are sent out to each and every artist showing up on that label's data research reports. I know this because I've received these types of emails, often with a ridiculous lowball offer attached to them.

What your job will now be is to field these emails and begin dialogues. You want to see who and what type of opportunities might resonate with you. This could be a huge range of possibilities—from the president of a huge, major label to a booking request at that venue or at a coffee shop in your local city.

Fire Creates More Fire

One thing is for certain. The more you do your job of turning your little spark into a five-alarm fire call, the more your inbox is going to be full *and* the more those people are going to desperately want to work with you.

Anything could happen, of course. Some of these people may want to offer you a deal immediately, or maybe they'll want to hear some more unreleased music or to meet with you in Los Angeles, NYC, or London. It's basically all about starting a rapport and seeing if there's a relationship.

By this time, you might already have a manager or an attorney, so no doubt you'll be looping them in to everything that's happening.

With every business relationship, especially with labels, there's a tipping point—when it just makes a whole hell of a lot of sense to say yes to the offer and the people involved. Similarly, sometimes it can make a whole lot of sense to say no. But when should you do that?

Let's Do This, Or Not

Deciding is different for everyone. The answer sometimes comes down to money—what is a life-changing amount? It could mean $30,000 so you can quit your Uber job to focus entirely on making music, or a dedicated $50,000 or $500,000 behind your project with the full support of a label. That monetary number could really be anything, but the offer and the money or advance are usually equal to the level of fire you've stoked and your business plan. In other words, don't expect a $100,000 label deal if you only generated $750 of master royalties over the last year. But hey, stranger things have happened.

Math Time—Do You Even Need a Label Deal?

Let's look at a quick-case label offer. You've released an album, and you're getting to the point where two of your songs just crossed one million Spotify streams. The other eight songs have between 250,000 to 750,000 streams each. How many streams is that? Let's say on average, those eight tracks have 500,000 streams each = four million streams. Add your other two tracks at one million streams each = six million streams total. Plug that number into the royalty calculator at www.StreamingRoyaltyCalculator.com and the value of your streams on the master side is about $24,000.

If a label offered you a deal for $25,000 at this point, and you've only collected $5,000 so far, is that a good deal for you? Probably not! Because if you just hang out for another nine to twelve months, that mailbox money is finally going to catch up to you. The label knows those royalties are out there, so even though an offer might come in at $25,000, the label's only risking about $6,000. Let me explain further:

The label knows you might have collected $5,000 so far and that even if nothing at all happens with your streaming, there's at least $19,000 still to come in, and the label advanced you $25,000.

  $25,000 (the advance)
\- $19,000 (incoming royalties)
= $6,000 risk money for the label

Keep in mind the label will end up owning a percentage (if not all) of your master as well. So yeah, I probably wouldn't do that deal.

Now, maybe that same situation *might* make a little more sense if a label (indie or major) says, "Okay, we'll give you $25,000 as an advance and another $25,000 on top of that to spend on digital marketing and promotion, and another $10,000 for a video budget for this album. That might start to look appealing, especially if it's a fifty-fifty-type income split. (Don't worry we'll also take a look at the million dollar offers too).

It's About the Relationships

Besides the money, as important, if not more important, is the benefit of that label's team, their hard work, their label muscle, and their relationships. This is huge.

At the end of the day, whom you decide to work with will be based on your evaluation of that company or individual person's level of relationships, and also on their expertise in executing. These executives often have deep relationships, some of which have extended twenty years or more. As an example,

- Can your champion at the label send just one text message and forever change your life?
- Does your new, future-label partner have an amazing relationship with someone who can perhaps get you a slot on Coachella?
- Does the company have great relationships with film supervisors?
- Do they have a great track record of breaking new artists?
- Do you like working with them and trust them to pay you all you've been promised?

All these conceptual and strategic points are crucial to consider on top of what you're getting paid for up front. There are so many books on how and when to do a label deal and what they should look like, so here I'm just giving you some broad strokes on when it might make sense to do a deal. Plus, you're going to have your team, ideally including a manager and an attorney, to help lead you in the right direction, so make sure you're fully consulting with them. In fact, at this point, they should definitely be taking the lead.

Major Labels = Math Time Part Deux

Obviously, if you get a massive million-dollar offer from say Republic or Universal, yeah, that's a deal you probably want to take. But let's be real. If you have that type of offer from one label, you probably have five other offers you'll be looking at too. On top of that, maybe the cash flow coming through the system is so amazing, you decide to continue doing things on your own. Literally, if you're a brand-new or established artist and have a catalog that's generating five million streams a week, that adds up to about $1,040,000 per year that you keep yourself. And that's not including all the income from synch uses, merchandise, touring, and tickets. The labels these days usually want a piece of all this. Of course, it's going to be all on you to set up, release, market, and promote everything.

There are lots of factors to look at. There are always tradeoffs and gives and takes.

The Hustle

Notwithstanding the preceding points, at the end of the day, picking the right people to work with, well, sometimes it just also comes down to:

a) Who is most passionate to work with you? Which label is going to work for you at 2 a.m. on a Sunday morning?

b) Do they have the relationships to take you to the next level?

c) What does your gut tell you?

All things being equal, or even if it's less, like in the case of an advance, I would go with less money if those elements in a, b, and c are all lighting up for you.

The other reason to do a deal with a label, particularly a major label, is if your music needs to be worked at commercial radio. This is something, at least in my experience, that you really can't do on your own. First, the cost per single is enormous—it can easily cost $500,000 for a commercial radio campaign. Secondly, it's really only the major labels who have the types of radio relationships and leverage needed to get your song to emerge on the radio charts.

Let's say you're a new artist and the major label is pitching you to the big radio station to add your song to their rotation. Often there are trades and/or legal quid pro quo. For instance, the major radio station might say, "Okay, we'll add your new artist to our rotation, but in return we want superstar XYZ to come and do a special holiday promotion with us." Done deal. That type of leverage or trade is just something you can't do on your own, unless you own your own label and have superstars on the roster....

We Don't Need No Stinkin' Fire

Speaking on a personal level, a situation might come along where you might even get an offer from We Are: The Guard, my indie label. (This scenario could be representative of many other types of indie labels or offers you might get.) Often at We Are: The Guard, we get involved a lot sooner in artists' careers.

Yes. We sign artists based on how good their music is and not necessarily how much fire there is.

If you have the music, the culture, the sonic and visual identity, the songs, the obsession, and the mindset I fully described in previous chapters, then we're interested. And if you have some type of following already, or a few tracks previously released that have done pretty good, that's the icing on the cake. If you don't have that, it's fine too. We just proceed with caution if we're starting from absolute zero. Like, if you need to push a car down the street, it's relatively easy once you get the car moving that first initial foot. Compare that to all the muscle power needed to get that car rolling from a dead standstill. The same holds true for new artists. It's always great if some type of groundwork and momentum has already been built.

That being said, when it comes to indie offers, we generally look at achievable targets. We want to at least break even on our investment and analyze what it's going to cost to get there. We then work backwards, coming up with a plan and a dedicated budget spend, which often includes a fund for

- videos,
- marketing and promotion,
- remixes,
- new recordings,
- publicity,
- influencer marketing,
- tour support, and
- other assets.

Our budget really just depends on the artist. And you accepting our offer isn't just about the budget, of course. As mentioned throughout the book, it's about having a team of experts who are uber passionate about your music and who will be tirelessly working for your dreams to come true, mining those deep relationships and putting in the midnight oil. (And in doing so, we're making our own dreams come true, which is to become the number-one indie pop label in the United States.)

The other part of the equation is about freeing up your time so you can focus on making that next hit, creating that next amazing recording, and perfecting your next single and EP, all while the label is doing all of that heavy lifting you used to do. A great label partner should also eliminate those 221 five-minute, soul-sucking jobs you had to do.

Questions and Answers You Need to Feel Right About

If you do get a label proposal—from my label or the biggest label on the planet, the following questions have to be asked along with subsequent great answers. No doubt, when I'm putting together my own proposal for artists to review, I'm also thinking from your perspective and if our answers tick the right boxes and make sense for everyone.

If your answers to the questions below are strong yesses, then it's likely a label deal worth signing with. However, if you have more than a few considerations, it's worth rethinking the offer, and at the very least furthering discussion with the label. It's always a negotiation, and it's worth having those open dialogues either yourself or absolutely, having your representatives do the talking if you those people on the team.

Yes or No

- Does the budget or advance substantially surpass your existing and immediate future cash flow?
- Does the label have the ability to level up and exponentiate what you're doing on your own?
- Will the label challenge you to be your best? Will they act as an inspiring coach who holds your growth and expertise at a level way above where you're currently at. Will they push you to be your best or be like "Cool. Nice song, bro. Let's try to win this game and yeah, see what happens." Big. Difference.
- Does the label have past wins and experience doing this?
- What's the label's reputation?
- Does the label get you and will they support your creative vision or do they just want to change your art?
- Will you have a champion at the label? What happens if that person leaves the label? (That's a good reason to sign to a label where the boss can't get fired, i.e., myself and my own label and publishing company.)
- Does it just feel right? Listen to your team members—your manager and attorney, but also to your gut.
- **What are the internal deal points?**

  It's not just about the money.

- Does this deal go on forever?
- What percentage of royalties do I get?
- What happens if I sign and we hate each other?
- What does this deal look like if suddenly there's massive success?

  (Quick note: If you sign a contract—and it's just not working out (for you or them, based on the original deal terms), labels and other professionals usually don't want to belabor a deal that isn't working. The good news is the great word "renegotiation." Trust me, if your project goes totally ballistic and exceeds all expectations, most labels recognize the value of a relationship and want to keep you happy. It's not uncommon to reward success with success, aka better deal points than what you signed on for.)

- Do I even like these people at the label, like my A&R point person, and do I think I'm going to have a blast and enjoy this experience?

  (This may seem like a small one vs. how much money you'll get, but if you and the label are both deep in the trenches fighting for each other, you're going to want to have the experience of working with someone you like and who has your back.)

When I send out my label deal proposals, I put myself in the shoes of the artist. I want to have all of the above questions answered with a resounding *yes* by the artists.

Summary

If you've done your job like I've discussed throughout the book, you might just have your inbox going nuts. Congrats! That's what you set out to accomplish. And you might have all kinds of different offers pouring in. Take a breath and get used to it.

There's always a time to do a label deal, and a time to educate yourself on what comes along with different label deals and structures. The more you create fire upon fire, the better your negotiating position and leverage will be.

A label will likely be the most critical member and component of your team, and they will take your career to the next level. Who knows, maybe our paths will cross in the future, and you'll end up seeing my name in your inbox wanting to hear more of your great music.

17

THE LAST NOTE

The summary of all summaries

Not every music executive sits down to write a book on how to sign yourself, giving you the tools, mindset, instruction, and experience on how to do it. But I'm so excited about supporting new artists that I really wanted to get all of this important, rarely circulated information in your hands. Maybe that's counterintuitive. Maybe most people want to hold on to this information, much less make the effort to put it all together, but really, I'm so pleased this book and the content within has found its way to your hands. And there is a good chance that if you're reading this, maybe it will cause synchronicity and our paths will cross in the future. Who knows, maybe if I didn't write this book, we'd never meet.

As a music executive for the last twenty-five years, I pride myself on early artist development and getting involved in their careers very early. Between my publishing company and my label, I often don't really need to see that fire or all those online data research reports, because I know amazing talent when I see and hear it. And I love nothing more than nurturing new artists and seeing their stars rise to the top. It's an amazing feeling.

I wish you all the best in using this information and these tools. I'd love to see you putting them to the most amazing use, changing your life, and ultimately changing those lives around you with the power of amazing music messages.

As I've mentioned before, this is not the end-all way to find your success. This is merely a guide and a handbook that will hopefully set you on the right course. It's about creating that spark, that ruckus and commotion through being yourself, creating the music you *need* to create, identifying and connecting with your first true thousand fans, and rinsing and repeating the process. Have that and both your inbox and your phone will start blowing up.

And like I said in the beginning of our journey—focus entirely and work first in finding your 1st true 1,000 fans. I'm confident that if you create that artistic specialness, and follow the premises within this book—you'll create that special fire and your amazing work to resonate.

So, what was that question, again? How do I get a record deal? No, Sign Yourself!

I wish you the very best of journeys.

Sincerely,

Benjamin Groff

www.BenjaminGroff.com
www.WeAreTheGuard.com
www.BrillBuilding.com

BONUS!

ESSENTIAL BOOKS AND BLOGS

And thought leaders to follow

I am a rabid book recommender of a few essential, life-changing books that can turn your world left, right, and upside down—for the better, of course. Below is a list of those who are, in my opinion, some of the best authors and great thinkers of the last hundred years. These blogs and books, in my professional career, have made a definitive night-and-day change in my approach to my life, and I really believe their principles and mindsets are essential if you're going to make it—not just in the music business, but in practically any endeavor.

Books

SETH GODIN[83]

Seth Godin deserves a whole chapter in this book. If you want to jump right into new modern strategies for marketing and standing out in the crowd, simply look no further than Seth. He's an amazing writer, and his thinking and unique outlook are essential on the subject. (If Seth ever reads this book, thank you, Seth, for all of the invaluable thoughts and leadership you've provided over the years.) All of Seth's techniques can be applied to the music business and promoting your art.

Seth's amazing daily blog is www.sethgodin.com. His TED convention talk "How to Get Your Ideas to Spread"[84] is one of my favorite presentations.

My favorite books by Seth:

Purple Cow: Transform Your Business by Being Remarkable

This is all about standing out in a crowd and being remarkable. All of my writers and artists know the purple cow language, and it's usually the first book I give them upon signing with me. *Purple Cow* changed my entire perspective about doing dangerous, important work and shipping art, and knowing that being just pretty good is the worst thing you can be in today's marketplace. You need to stand out. In every way. Period.

Permission Marketing: Turning Strangers into Friends and Friends into Customers

Permission marketing is not a push model; it's called a pull model, enabling your fans to spread the word via anticipated, permission-based, and relative messages that your fans are delighted with and waiting to receive from you.

Linchpin: Are You Indispensable?

You'll find at least one big idea in this book that you can apply to your own artistry. It's also an economy book and talks about how things have drastically changed and how they're also never coming back. You'll find the answers on how to thrive and find opportunity in today's disruption.

If you're only going to get one book. I would say jump right now to get *Purple Cow.* You'll thank me later.

RYAN HOLIDAY

Perennial Seller: The Art of Making and Marketing Work that Lasts

I've bought twenty copies of this book just to hand out; it's literally that good. Ryan Holiday dissects what it takes to create a perennial seller—that book, movie, or song that stays in the charts or as a top seller forever.

Ryan really dissects the concept in the book and will provide you with a new mindset to accomplish this. The most important and eye-opening part of the book was the marketing section.

DON PASSMAN

All You Need to Know About the Music Business

This is the definitive bible on the music business. It's a great read, especially if you are actually starting to get calls from the labels. There's no better book on the subject than what Don has written here. He's also one of the world's biggest and most powerful music attorneys, so he definitely knows what he's talking about.

NAPOLEON HILL

Think and Grow Rich

An essential idea of the book is you need to believe full-heartedly that you deserve the success and wealth you're setting out for, but you first need to be the person who will effortlessly attract that success. The premise here is:

BE > DO > HAVE. The rest will follow.

MALCOLM GLADWELL[85]

Outliers: The Story of Success

This book gives an amazing insight into the idea of putting in your ten thousand hours to succeed. Yes, ten thousand hours! Malcolm Gladwell has figured out that any amazing accomplished artist, musician, CEO, or champion hockey player has put in at least ten thousand hours of work and practice and experience before they really breakthrough, and he gives numerous examples of the results.

The big takeaway here is simple—putting in the time and the work is crucial.

The Tipping Point: How Little Things Can Make a Big Difference

Gladwell presents that with every big breakthrough, there was usually a tipping point, pushing it over the edge to where the bigger audience finally got it. There are fascinating chapters on how to share your visions or artistic product with the right people. Who are your connectors who can spread the word to their credible community and create your tipping point?

Go-To Music Industry Directories

The Music Registry

This is the industry reference/contact bible and most complete up-to-date and reliable directory for the music business. You can order a hard copy or a downloadable database of record labels; music publishing executives; film, TV, and music supervisors; and music attorneys. Accept no imitations, because they'll just be copying these resources. If you're going to reach out to anyone on the lists and pitch your music, remember all of the guidelines previously outlined in this book!

Essential Blogs to Follow

A very short list of people whose thoughts may be essential to add to your world.

The Lefsetz Letter[86]

Bob Lefsetz is a no-holds-barred music analyst floating around in the top and bottom levels of the music industry. You'll get an unedited and sometimes too-honest view of what's going on for real in the music world. Without Bob's insight, I simply wouldn't be positioned where I am today. Bob also publishes positive and negative input from today's leading executives, industry shakers, and artists themselves.

Visit and sign up for *The Lefsetz Letter* right now!

A VC in NY[87]

This is Fred Wilson's blog, the co-owner of Union Square Ventures and a major tech investor. Lucky for us, he's also a music fan, and in this blog you'll get instant early insights on technology—where things are heading and what's on the horizon. Fred was an early investor in Kickstarter, Twitter, FourSquare, and key crypto companies. He knows his stuff, so use it to enhance your own music and exposure.

Seth Godin

Again, you can get a daily post from Seth giving you at least one great idea that you can apply to your own project, which might just create your own tipping point.

Derek Sivers[88]

This is the site of Derek Sivers, super-cool human, musician/artist, founder of CD Baby, good guy to all musicians and artists, and a personal friend.

Derek is a self-starting, self-made guy who always delivers from the heart. He ended up selling CD Baby for about twenty million bucks, but he's still very committed to serving and doing things for artists and musicians. Derek's website and books are chockfull of valuable, fantastic, and inspirational information.

Benjamin Groff[89]

Yeah, it's me—that guy whose book you're reading right now. I've been in the music business for twenty-five years—mostly via music publishing, with my signings (admitted bragging coming) generating over $125 million in publishing revenue.

I've been posting my cumulative and uncommon knowledge, from secrets of hit songwriting to mindset to new marketing approaches, and so much more. I literally think there's a million dollars' worth of information there, if you put the ideas, concepts, and principles to work.

Plus, of course, you can sign up for one of my online courses.

Summary

There are amazing thinkers and thought leaders out there. Hardly any of them are writing specifically about music, but all of their books and blogs contain pearls of wisdom, new ways of thinking, mindset rewiring, and education that will become invaluable in your journey. Embrace as much learning as you can from them, and happy reading.

ACKNOWLEDGEMENTS

I wouldn't have been able to write this book if it weren't for so many special people who've been mentors, supporters, and believers.

In no particular order, but to start: my parents for supporting me in the beginning to take a shot in this crazy music business, and to take the uncommon path that others in our little 250-person hometown thought was just nuts.

To my great teachers and professors along the way: Tom Strohman and Jeff Charles in Lebanon, PA; and at Berklee College of Music: Jack Perricone, Sir Pat Pattison, and Bonnie Hayes. Molly Kaye, for giving me my very first shot with a paid job in the music business. If it wasn't for us running into each other at Extreme's rehearsal space twenty-five years ago (adjacent to that donut factory in Somerville), who knows where I'd be. Maybe making donuts. Holly Greene, Clyde Lieberman, and Danny Strick for also being great bosses, teachers and supporters. Jody Gerson, for showing me how to put together and analyze deals, and for allowing me to sit across your desk for an hour a week and learn how an operator operates.

To my other coaches and mentors who've allowed me to grow and your transfer of uncommon knowledge: Neil Strauss, Dan Sullivan at Strategic Coach, and Ryan Soave. To the Kobalt team who've made it all happen, both in nurturing myself and my company and helping me to recoup my deals: Sas Metcalfe, Richard Sanders, Laurent Hubert, Jacob Paul, Jeannette Perez, and the entire Kobalt synch team (who do *the* very best work in the music business), Amanda Samii, Jamie Kineleski, Sue Drew, Sean Dishman, and Anna Schlafer.

And, of course, my team at Brill Building and We Are: The Guard: Tyler Johnson, Robin Hansel, Arielle Tindel and Beca Arredondo. And certainly, all the great writers and artists I've been fortunate to work with over the years.

Last, but certainly not least, Willard Ahdritz for your rock star genius, generosity, mentorship, and friendship, and for retransforming the music business. Where would we be without you? I like it!

Anyone would be humbled and grateful to have these people in one's life.

ABOUT THE AUTHOR

Benjamin Groff was a dual major in songwriting and performance at Berklee College of Music from 1989–1993. His career in music publishing extends over twenty-five years, including working at BMG Music Publishing (bought by Universal) and EMI Music Publishing (bought by Sony), as well as being the first US employee of Kobalt Music Publishing, where he helped build the Kobalt roster over ten years as Executive VP of Creative. Benjamin is currently the owner of his own publishing company, Brill Building, as well as label and music filter, We Are: The Guard.

Benjamin's signings range from Ryan Tedder, Kelly Clarkson, The Lumineers, Grimes, Savan Kotecha, OneRepublic, SOPHIE, Ariel Rechtshaid, Greg Kurstin, Tiesto, Kid Cudi, Ariel Pink, TOKiMONSTA, TR/ST, Cut Copy, Big Freedia, Lindy Robbins, Peaches, and yes, even Steel Panther.

His specialty in the music business is early artist, writer and writer/producer development.

How Do I Get a Record Deal? Sign Yourself! is Benjamin's first book. He also provides an abundance of content on his songwriting-based music blog at BenjaminGroff.com. He has a number of songwriting and marketing courses available at the website, providing uncommon wisdom, knowledge, and teachings which he's accumulated over his career.

Outside of the music business, Benjamin is an avid learner, spending much time in self-development, biohacking, as well as continually taking part in adventurous and challenging trainings and programs (some of these are sworn to secrecy). He enjoys amazing hikes, exploring remote nature, options and futures trading, seeing the world, amazing filmmakers (Morricone, Kurosawa, Jodorowsky, Tarrantino), 60s-80s sports cars (I'm coming for you, 1969 Detomaso Mangusta) and continuing his deep connoisseur dives into high- and low-brow culture, while at the end of the day helping others be the very best they can be.

WORK WITH ME!

You've made it to the end of the book, or maybe you just completely cheated and skipped to the last page, which is perfectly fine too. This is the place where I tell you a little more about how you can work directly with me, submit your music, correspond, or even get personal coaching.

Who knows, maybe I'll discover that you're the next big artist, songwriter, or producer, and we'll end up working together. While that might happen, one more immediate way we can further connect is by reaching out through a number of platforms, all of which I've mentioned throughout the book.

Submitting Your Music for Review

If you have a song that you can't wait to share with the world and would like feedback and advice, you can submit the song to me on my Fluence profile.[90] I usually write about one to three hundred words of feedback and advice. And who knows, maybe one of those sentences will have an impact on your song, or maybe even overall artist direction.

As I've mentioned, Fluence is a site where you can find a multitude of experts to review your artistry, and you pay them for their time. While my hourly rate is high, you're only paying for my time to listen to your song, so most submissions cost between $12–$15 USD. Not bad.

I don't have time to listen to songs for free, but Fluence is an excellent tool whereby artists and songwriters can get constructive feedback and thoughts, as well focused attention.

Personal 1:1 Songwriting and Artist Coaching

Including advice on releasing your music and on music business items from labels, publishing, managers, attorneys, deals, etc.

If you have some burning questions about your artist and/or songwriting career, or you want advice on a deal you're thinking about, ideas on your marketing plan, deep dives and critiquing on specific songs, or anything else to do with a music career, you can hire me at an hourly rate on Upwork.[91]

My hourly rate is not cheap here, but it's probably cheaper than it would cost to get some instant answers on your art, direction, contracts from an entertainment lawyer, who charges at least $350 an hour.

LEARN MORE!

Courses

I'm offering a number of digital courses that I'm extremely excited about. You can get more information about them on my website.[92] At the time of writing, there should at least be one course launched and more forthcoming. Check it out, as I think there's about a million bucks of potential info for your artist career within the courses. And don't worry that it's all just a repeat of what's in this book. It's all new, fresh material.

Insider Secrets of Hit Songwriting

Get the unfair advantage of all my juiciest, best stuff! This course has over eight hours of content focused on what makes hit songs tick—in any genre, in any decade. There's a ton of uncommon knowledge and theories that either I've created and/or that I've picked up from rare sources that I just don't hear about anywhere else. One of the modules alone, I would say, is worth as much as my entire Berklee College of Music tuition, it's that important.

With every course purchase, you'll also have the opportunity to get a deep discount of my personal time for a one-on-one critique session, or use the time to discuss whatever you'd like, e.g., artist direction, music business, or marketing strategy.

I could try to describe the core material of the course, but honestly, a lot of the presentations are deep dives into each subject category. I *can* say, without a doubt, that all the key hitmakers today, as well as the classic songwriters who've made hits in any genre, in any decade, are using these elements in their hit song creations. The course is a full cumulation of my experience in publishing. Much of this emanates from having heard over fifty thousand unreleased songs and/or artists that never made it past go when compared to those songs that just zoom to the top of the charts. Feel free to check out some key previews on my site.[93]

The Release Blueprint—Music Marketing Strategies

How to Get Your First One Million Streams

In this course, I take you through a point-by-point, week-by-week, and day-by-day release rollout plan. This is the exact same plan we use for my label We Are: The Guard, which has garnered over two hundred million streams!

You've made your great art; now, it's time to roll out your release and share it with the world. The course provides seventy-five individual, detailed video modules including the steps, tips, and instructions on not just how to do something, but also when. The plan starts with your product six weeks out from your release date—with actions you need to take for that week, all the way up to release date—when the release items start moving quicker in a day-to-day process. After the release date, there are several post-release ideas and plans you can implement to add to your strategy. This doesn't mean that every step is for you. This overall plan is our own starting point for each release, so once you have the blueprint open, you can go through the entire process and see which strategies and items are really pertinent to you as an artist.

This course will let me help you:

a) make sure you have a step-by-step guide and have the right release plan for your important piece of art,

b) stand out from the crowd among the thirty to fifty thousand song releases coming out per day, and

c) avoid all the pitfalls and mistakes that I've personally made with my own money.

If the sticker price is a little spendy for you, there's an easy payment plan option. This course will put you in the slipstream and give you a repeatable process you can use for each and every release, so it'll pay for itself many times over. Your course subscription will also give you access to all the updates I provide. As the music business evolves so quickly, there's always a new way of doing something, and I'll be updating the modules along the way.

Lastly, as provided earlier in the book, feel free to get the current release rollout plan for We Are: The Guard.[94] This is just a preview of what the course looks like, with full details and how-tos for each of these steps along the way. Feel free to check out some the key previews of the Release Blueprint course, and you can find that on my website.[95]

LEGAL DISCLAIMER

The text and content of this book is the personal opinion of Benjamin Groff on behalf of BitCrush.FM, Inc. The content provided is for informational purposes only, you should not construe any such information or other material as specific career, legal, tax, investment, financial, or other advice, whether be it based on life or career decisions. It is very important to do your own analysis before making any decisions based on your own personal circumstances. Methods described and discussed in this book change rapidly. You should take independent advice from a professional representative in connection with, or independently research and verify, any information that has been presented and which to rely upon, whether for the purpose of making a career decision or otherwise. Past performance is not a guarantee of future results, nor is it necessarily indicative of future performance.

We have done our best to ensure that the information provided in this book, audio book and the resources are accurate, however we can not be held liable or accountable for any mistakes, errors or opinions. The author and publisher hold no responsibilities for any specific outcomes. Regardless of anything to the contrary, nothing through this book or audio book should be understood as a recommendation that you should not consult with a professional to address further particular information.

ENDNOTES

[1] Andy Hertzfeld, "Real Artists Ship," January 1984, http://www.folklore.org/StoryView.py?story=Real_Artists_Ship.txt.

[2] Check out and subscribe to Bob's essential blog, *The Lefsetz Letter*, at http://lefsetz.com/wordpress.

[3] Find out more at www.gratitudetraining.com.

[4] Read more about essential books and blogs I recommend in Bonus chapter at the end of the book.

[5] See more on this in Malcolm Gladwell's great book, *Outliers: The Story of Success* (New York: Little, Brown, 2008).

[6] I would encourage you to read this blog post, no matter if you are a hardcore jazz head, a Joni Mitchell singer-songwriter, or an indie rocker: "What Max Martin Knows That You Don't and Why You Should Adopt the Max Martin Mindset" at www.benjamingroff.com/blog/what-max-martin-knows-that-you-dont-and-why-you-should-adopt-the-max-martin-mindset.

[7] Upfluence has now expanded its influencer reach to TikTok as well.

[8] Seth Godin, *Purple Cow* (New York: Penguin, 2003), 45.

[9] Digital service providers like Apple, Spotify, Amazon, Tidal, Google Play.

[10] A reference to Seth Godin's *Purple Cow*.

[11] Check out his Wiki page, https://en.wikipedia.org/wiki/Spike_Jonze.

[12] OK Go, "Here It Goes Again," February 26, 2009, http://youtu.be/dTAAsCNK7RA.

[13] OK Go, "This Too Shall Pass – Rube Goldberg Machine," March 1, 2010, https://youtu.be/qybUFnY7Y8w.

[14] Spice Girls, "Wannabe," UMG (on behalf of Virgin Records Ltd), March 6, 2009, www.youtube.com/watch?v=gJLIiF15wjQ.

[15] Matt and Kim, "Let's Go," UMG, [Merlin] Liberation Music June 24, 2012, www.youtube.com/watch?v=zOylJn7uNVM.

[16] Matt and Kim, "Hey Now," Harvest Records, February 10, 2015, www.youtube.com/watch?v=zUslXuCNRi0.

[17] Matt and Kim, "It's Alright," FADER, UMG, [Merlin] Liberation Music, February 25, 2013, www.youtube.com/watch?v=PilVAqMMSnc.

[18] Ibeyi, "River," August 7, 2014, XL Recordings, www.youtube.com/watch?v=lHRAPlwsS5I.

[19] Kiesza, "Hideway," April 25, 2014, Island Records, www.youtube.com/watch?v=Vnoz5uBEWOA.

[20] Wax, "California," directed by Spike Jonze, UMG; Interscope, August 10, 2012, https://www.youtube.com/watch?v=U5vzJZHc59s.

[21] Matt and Kim, "Lessons Learned," WMG, UMG (on behalf of FADER), February 29, 2012, www.youtube.com/watch?v=xLaKE2eeeXM.

[22] Dirty Vegas, "Days Go By," November 21, 2018, www.youtube.com/watch?v=gLCduDJVksc.

[23] Sick Puppies, "Free Hugs Campaign," September 22, 2006, https://youtu.be/vr3x_RRJdd4.

[24] YouTube Help, "How Content ID works," accessed December 29, 2019, www.youtube.com/t/contentid.

[25] Young Thug, "Wyclef Jean," WMG (on behalf of Atlantic Records), www.youtube.com/watch?v=_9L3j-lVLwk.

[26] Jessie J, "Mamma Knows Best," UMG (on behalf of Lava Music/Republic Records), July 9, 2009, www.youtube.com/watch?v=TswOLHUQFPk.

[27] boburnham, "I'm bo yo." June 17, 2008, https://youtu.be/Z-ap5Fp2T6c.

[28] PomplamooseMusic," "Single Ladies (Put a Ring on It) - Beyonce," September 17, 2009, https://www.youtube.com/watch?v=oIr8-f2OWhs

[29] Macromedia Inc.

[30] Justin Bieber, "The Star of Stratford, Canada," October 7, 2007, www.youtube.com/watch?v=28VmUxTDU5Q.

[31] Iamamiwhoami, "15.6.6.9.3.9.14.1.18.21.13.56155," February 22, 2010, https://youtu.be/UxC4zMCwefo.

[32] TOBACCO, "Human Om," [Merlin] SC Distribution (on behalf of Ghostly International), July 11, 2016, https://www.youtube.com/watch?v=facG8Lyv3Yk.

[33] Ray-Ban Films, "Sunglass Catch," May 6, 2007, http://youtu.be/-prfAENSh2k.

[34] http://www.topspinmedia.com. I am not sure how active TopSpin is currently.

[35] Mike Masnick, "Nine Inch Nails Sells Out Of $300 Deluxe Edition In Under Two Days," *Techdirt*, March 4, 2008, http://www.techdirt.com/articles/20080304/162842435.shtml.

[36] Michael Masnick, "Michael Masnick The Trent Reznor case study," February 3, 2009, https://www.youtube.com/watch?v=Njuo1puB1lg.

[37] http://www.wearetheguard.com/

[38] https://www.awal.com/

[39] http://www.streamingroyaltycalculator.com

[40] Hallywoodone, "Arsenio Hall (Hmmmmm Mix)," March 18, 2010, https://www.youtube.com/watch?v=jzzGjCmABzw.

[41] http://www.brillbuilding.com/

[42] http://www.kobaltmusic.com/

[43] https://www.tunecore.com

[44] https://distrokid.com

[45] https://cdbaby.com

[46] While Derek was running the company, you really could tell that this place was a totally different kind of company that truly cared, which is unique in the often-anonymous world of digital companies, or any company, for that matter. I highly encourage you to check out Derek Sivers' website, www.sivers.org. Derek is an exceptional thought leader and author, and I'm pleased to be able to call him a friend. Check out his books too: https://sivers.org.

[47] https://stem.is

[48] https://www.human-re-sources.com

[49] Ben Sisario, "A New Spotify Initiative Makes the Big Record Labels Nervous," September 6, 2018, *The New York Times* online,

www.nytimes.com/2018/09/06/business/media/spotify-music-industry-record-labels.html.

[50] https://www.theorchard.com

[51] https://aristakeacademy.teachable.com/p/streaming-instagram-growth

[52] http://www.hypem.com

[53] http://www.fluence.io/benjamingroff

[54] I wrote a whole in-depth blog post about it that you can read here: https://www.benjamingroff.com/blog/why-your-live-show-sucks-pt-1.-you-got-no-show-in-your-live-show

[55] https://www.benjamingroff.com/blog/why-your-live-show-sucks-pt-1.-you-got-no-show-in-your-live-show

[56] https://www.motherfalcon.com

[57] https://trello.com

[58] www.benjamingroff.com/release

[59] Look them up on Spotify or Apple or YouTube.

[60] www.upwork.com

[61] Here's an example of a lyric video I paid $150 for and has over three million YouTube streams: www.youtube.com/watch?v=eUT49JWxiz8.

[62] If you want to hire me for creative coaching on Upwork, www.upwork.com/o/profiles/users/_~01e36b6daa7af00a5a/

[63] www.fiverr.com

[64] www.creative-commission.com

[65] To date, our label has had about eight Spotify New Music Friday playlist adds. I can't describe what a thrill it is when that happens!

[66] https://artists.spotify.com

[67] We've discussed what a one-sheet is previously, and we've also included some one-sheet examples in the appendix. Just jump to the end of the book if you'd like to see what ours look like.

[68] https://www.instagram.com/mxmsisdead/?hl=en

[69] Seth Godin, *Permission Marketing: Turning Strangers into Friends and Friends into Customers* (New York: Simon & Schuster, 1999).

[70] New York: Simon & Schuster, 2019.

[71] www.benjamingroff.com/blog

[72] I only just picked this thought up via Zig Ziglar's famous *Secrets of Closing the Sale* (Grand Rapids: Revell, 2006).

[73] *We Are: The Guard* is my own music blog.

[74] *The Jerk*, directed by Carl Reiner (Universal City, CA: Universal Pictures, 1979), DVD.

[75] https://songspace.com

[76] https://soundcloud.com

[77] https://www.box.com

[78] https://www.dropbox.com

[79] I also recommend reading essential sales books like Robert B. Cialdini's *Influence: The Power of Persuasion* (New York: William P. Morrow, 1993)

and basically anything and everything by Zig Ziglar, the godfather to a few of my heroes like Seth Godin and Tony Robbins.

[80] https://www.google.com/alerts

[81] https://www.brillbuilding.com/roster

[82] https://www.musicregistry.com

[83] https://www.sethgodin.com/#books-courses-and-more

[84] https://youtu.be/xBIVlM435Zg

[85] www.gladwellbooks.com/landing-page/malcolm-gladwell-books/

[86] https://www.lefsetz.com

[87] https://avc.com

[88] https://sivers.org

[89] https://www.benjamingroff.com

[90] https://fluence.io/benjamingroff

[91] https://www.benjamingroff.com/coach

[92] https://www.benjamingroff.com/courses

[93] https://www.benjamingroff.com/secrets

[94] PDF release plan

[95] https://www.benjamingroff.com/release

Made in the USA
Middletown, DE
21 August 2022